Unbeaten

How biblical heroes rose above
their pain... and you can too.

LINDSEY BELL

CrossRiver

BREWSTER, KANSAS USA

To Keith.
Our life hasn't turned out exactly as I planned it,
but I wouldn't want to do life with anyone else.
We are unbeaten… together.

CONTENTS

Acknowledgments

T o my husband, *Keith,* who walked with me through each of our miscarriages, as well as every other difficult situation I've gone through in my adult life. Thank you for carrying me through the hard times.

To my boys, *Rylan* and *Caden.* I know there were days in the midst of my grief I wasn't the best mother to you two. Thank you for loving me anyway. Thank you for giving me a reason to keep on smiling and laughing.

To *Eden, Jesse, Ella,* and *Jadon.* Though I never met you on this earth, I can't wait until the day I get to meet you in heaven. Your lives, though way too short, have changed mine. I'm a better person because of the months I carried each of you.

To my parents, *Chuck* and *Eve Poznich,* who put a tree in their backyard in honor of all of their grandbabies, even the ones they never got to meet. Mom, when we lost that first baby, you were there. I still remember what you did when I told you the news. You didn't offer advice or tell me it would be okay. Instead, you cried with me and hugged me. Thank you. It was exactly what I needed.

To my brothers, *Jason* and *Jared,* and my sister-in-law, *Kayla.* Thank you for loving me through my pain.

To my *critique group,* thank you for taking time to make sure I got rid of the unnecessary "thats" and other pet words. You ladies bless my heart.

To you, my *readers.* Thank you for picking up this book. It is because of you — and the hope my difficulties can somehow help you — that I write.

Most importantly, to *God,* for making me whole again. I might not be the same person I was when I first lost a baby, but I'm not broken anymore... all because of You.

Introduction

Boxing gloves on the cover of a devotional and Bible study? Sure, it might seem a little odd at first. But if you think about it, it makes sense.

There is nothing our enemy enjoys more than throwing punches at us. These punches often come in the form of health crises, marriage conflicts, job loss, death, abandonment, divorce, and a variety of other painful life circumstances.

The battle we face is real. Many of us have scars to prove it. But the fight isn't over yet. Because you've picked up this book, I know you've still got fight in you. One of the best ways to fight the enemy is by doing what Jesus did in Matthew 4. When Satan tempted Jesus, Jesus used Scripture to block the punches. That's what we'll do in this study.

Romans 15:4 says "everything that was written in the past was written to teach us, so that through the endurance taught in the Scriptures and the encouragement they provide we might have hope."

For the next ten weeks, we'll dig into the Scriptures together and use what was written in the past to help us with today. Like Jesus did in the desert, we'll block Satan's punches using the Words of God and the hope they provide.

This ten-week Bible study and devotional is designed for you to use alone or with a small group. Each week contains five daily devotionals for you to read throughout the week by yourself. These devotionals include:

- Questions for reflection
- A prayer
- Scriptures for further meditation
- A journal activity to complete each day

At the back of the book is a study guide that can be used in a group setting at the end of each week.

To prepare for this study, purchase a journal (or grab one you already own) to use as you read. In your journal, record everything God teaches you. Record the answers to the questions for reflection as well as anything else God brings to mind as you read.

If you're doing this study with a group of friends or family members, plan to get together at the end of each week to watch a short video and discuss the study guide questions at the back of this book.

Are you ready to pick up your boxing gloves and get started?

Let's do this.

When Difficulties Come

I n this world you will have trouble." Jesus knew what He was talking about in John 16:33, didn't He? If you're reading this book, my guess is, you're going through something. Something that possibly makes you wonder where God is in your mess. Maybe you wonder why a God who claims to adore you is allowing this trial into your life. Or maybe you doubt He's really able to help because if He were able, He would, right?

There are no easy answers to these questions, and this book won't pretend there are. But it will do something else. It will remind you of what biblical heroes did in the past when they faced difficulties, and it will challenge you to follow in their footsteps.

You don't have to allow your pain to swallow your joy. You, too, can be unbeaten. You can, like Paul did in 2 Corinthians 4:9, say with confidence, "I might be struck down, but I am *not* destroyed."

For week one, we'll look at what several biblical heroes did when difficulties came their way. We'll start with Adam and Eve, the very first people who faced pain. Then we'll move on to Naomi, Job, Peter, Paul, and Silas.

After you complete this week's lessons, please watch the video at...

www.crossrivermedia.com/portfolio/unbeaten-week-one

Adam and Eve

Scripture reading: Genesis 4:1–12

"Now Cain said to his brother Abel, 'Let's go out to the field.' While they were in the field, Cain attacked his brother Abel and killed him." — Genesis 4:8

My husband and I prayed and believed God would step in and help. We had faith He was not only capable of fixing our problem, but also willing.

For whatever reason, though, God didn't. He didn't come to our rescue when we needed Him most, or more accurately, He didn't show up in the way we thought He would.

Have you been there? Maybe it was after a heated argument with your spouse. You prayed God would soften his heart toward you and instead got divorce papers and a letter telling you he was done.

Or maybe it was after an appointment with your doctor. You felt confident God would heal the cancer, but instead received bad news. The cancer had spread. Quite possibly it was after a job loss, death in the family, health crisis, or relationship strain.

For my husband and me, it was after a long and painful struggle with secondary infertility.[1] We endured four miscarriages in two years and walked away from each of these more and more discouraged. We struggled to understand why a God who was able to help chose not to.

In our minds, we were the only ones facing such a difficult trial. After all, when we talked with friends at church or at work, their lives seemed much easier than ours. We knew no one who had gone through as many miscarriages as we had. In contrast, most people we knew had no problem getting — or staying — pregnant. We felt alone, like no one else could possibly understand our pain.

It was this feeling of aloneness that led me to search God's Word. I knew there had to be something in there to help me know what to do to move forward with my life in the midst of heartache.

The first people I read about in the book of Genesis were Adam and Eve. On the sixth day of creation, after God fashioned the sun, earth, plants, and animals, He then made man and woman. Everything went well for a time, but then Adam and Eve chose to disobey God. Their disobedience flung them into a much more difficult world.

In Genesis 4, they faced one of the most difficult trials a parent can ever face: the death of a child. What's worse, their son Cain caused the death. He murdered his brother Abel because he was jealous God liked Abel's offering more than his own. Adam and Eve, in essence, lost two children that day: Abel, who was murdered, but also Cain, who was banished because of his sin.

As I read this story, I realized something. Pain has been around for a long time. In fact, it has been around since the very first people walked on earth. Though my trials are different than theirs (and I am sure most of yours are too), we are not alone in our pain. There are others who have walked before us who are familiar with tears, just as we are.

In this devotional, we'll look at many of these people. In the pages ahead, we'll study the lives of Job, Peter, Jesus, Hannah, Paul, Daniel, David, and Joseph to name a few. Some of these biblical heroes faced death. Others faced imprisonment or torture. All of them faced heartache. Suffering didn't begin with us. It began with Adam and Eve and will continue until Jesus comes back again.

Yes, pain is inevitable, but defeat is not. As you read this book, one thing you'll see over and over again is that most of the biblical figures were eventually victorious over their trials. Sometimes that victory came on this side of heaven. Other times, it came after they passed through heaven's gates.

In Romans, Paul describes those who endure hardships with their faith intact. "Who shall separate us from the love of Christ? Shall trouble or hardship or persecution or famine or nakedness or danger or sword? As it is written: 'For your sake we face death all day long; we are considered as sheep to be slaughtered.' No, in all these things we are more than conquerors through him who loved us." (Rom. 8:35-37)

That is my hope for you and me… that we would be more than conquerors through Him who saved us. That we would be victorious over our pain and triumphant in the end. That we would — no matter what comes our way — be unbeaten.

QUESTIONS FOR REFLECTION

1. What difficult circumstance(s) led you to this book?
2. How do you think Adam and Eve were able to continue with their lives after such a painful event?
3. What other biblical figures went through painful circumstances? (We'll look at many of these in the pages ahead!)

SCRIPTURES FOR FURTHER MEDITATION

Hebrews 11:32–40, Romans 8:22–23, 1 Peter 5:8–9

PRAYER

Pray God would use this study to minister to your heart. Ask Him to remind you of things and guide you as you dig into His Word.

JOURNAL ACTIVITY

Write in your journal the answer to the following question: What is your goal for reading this book?

TAKEAWAY

When difficulties come, know you're not alone.

Naomi

Scripture reading: Ruth 1:1–5, 20–21

*"'Don't call me Naomi,' she told them.
'Call me Mara, because the Almighty has made
my life very bitter. I went away full, but the Lord
has brought me back empty. Why call me Naomi?
The Lord has afflicted me; the Almighty has
brought misfortune upon me.'" — Ruth 1:20–21*

A few years ago, we had a miserable winter. I'm accustomed to the Midwest's cold winter months. I'm also used to a little bit of snow. An inch or two every couple of weeks isn't abnormal. But this particular winter was something unlike anything I had ever experienced. Some areas around my hometown received nearly two feet of snow. My children and I didn't leave our home for over a week. The local news anchors even referred to this storm as "The Snowpocalypse."

The snow was beautiful… at first. But anyone with young children can tell you enough is enough. By the third day, I despised the snow. My kids and I were antsy to leave the house, but the bitter winds made it unthinkable to play outside. Plus, the snow wasn't pretty anymore. What used to be white was now brown and coated with dirt. The sun could not melt it quickly enough.

Eventually, though, when the snow did melt and the earth began to warm with the approaching spring, I noticed something. The flowers were brighter than I had ever seen before. The colors, magnificent. The scents, heavenly.

Since then, I've learned about vernalization, the process by which cold weather promotes flowering. In essence, it's the miserable snow that makes the flowers so beautiful. If not for the months of winter and cold weather, those flowers wouldn't have been as pretty.

Isn't that often the case with us too? It's the long, hard, painful seasons that come before the blessings. It's the nastiness of winter that reminds us of the beauty of spring.

That is certainly what happened with Naomi. She lost her husband and children while living in a land far from home. She had no one left except her two daughters-in-law, and even they were foreigners. Can you blame her for growing bitter? Nearly everyone she loved was gone. Nearly everything she knew was a distant memory. Naomi asked those around her to stop calling her Naomi and to call her bitter instead.

Though Naomi's bitterness was understandable given her circumstances, Naomi forgot about one important part of her story: God. She failed to see how He could turn anything around. In her mind, there was no hope. God had failed her, so why bother Him anymore?

Have you ever felt this way? Have you lost hope God could — or would — redeem your situation? I have. After our third miscarriage, I stopped praying for a time. Why pray if God's not listening? What I failed to see in those months was that God wasn't done with my story yet. I'll tell you more about how God redeemed our miscarriages later, but know this today. God can — and will — redeem your story. God isn't done with you yet, just as He wasn't done with Naomi.

God still had some redeeming to do in Naomi's life. Even though her situation certainly appeared hopeless, God brought someone to restore some of what she had lost. Boaz married Naomi's daughter-in-law Ruth and then bore them a son.

A new child and son-in-law didn't replace the ones she lost. One life can never replace another. Even so, I'm convinced this was one of the ways God brought a flower from a harsh winter. God restored Naomi's loss — and gave her joy again. He can do the same for us, because God is in the business of restoring.

Even the Israelites in the Old Testament, who caused many of their problems with their disobedience to God, were restored. I love this quote from Deuteronomy 30:3: "Then the LORD your God will restore your fortunes and have compassion on you and gather you again from all the nations where he scattered you."

In the Old Testament, the Israelites often rebelled against God. Because of their rebellion, God allowed them to be captured by their enemies. He refused to leave them there, though. Time and time again, God came to their rescue and restored their brokenness. He redeemed their story, because our God is a God who restores. First Peter 5:10 puts it this way, "And the God of all grace, who called you to his eternal glory in Christ, after you have suffered a little while, will himself restore you and make you strong, firm and steadfast."

Today, God can — and will — restore our lives.

QUESTIONS FOR REFLECTION

1. In what way did God restore the things Naomi lost?

2. Do you believe God can restore your life as well? Why or why not?

3. Sometimes, God doesn't seem to fix things on this side of heaven. How do you reconcile this with the story of Naomi and others like it where it seems God redeems a negative situation?

PRAYER

Pray for God to remind you of the promises in the Bible. When you begin to feel bitterness creeping into your heart, ask God to restore your joy.

SCRIPTURES FOR FURTHER MEDITATION

1 Peter 5:10, Joel 2:23–27

JOURNAL ACTIVITY

Draw a picture of a flower and write beside it, "The prettiest flowers follow long winters." Look up Joel 2:25. How do the words, "I will repay you for the years the locusts have eaten," relate to Naomi's story and to yours?

TAKEAWAY

When difficulties come, trust God to restore.

Job

Scripture reading: Job 1:1–22

*"The LORD gave and the LORD has taken away;
may the name of the LORD be praised." — Job 1:21*

Yesterday my husband came home from work a few minutes early so I could go to a doctor's appointment without my children at my side. He arrived home at 4:00 and had an evening meeting at 6:00, so I knew he would need to finish dinner before I got home if he wanted to eat before the meeting. Being the thoughtful wife I am, at least on this day, I began dinner earlier and left it in the refrigerator.

As I walked out the door, I gave him what I thought were clear instructions. "I already started dinner. The noodles and vegetables are ready in the fridge. All you'll need to make is the sauce."

"Okay, hon. Thanks."

Since he answered me, I assumed he heard what I said. That was my first mistake: assuming something. My second mistake was saying something about the noodles when I arrived home and saw a fresh batch on the stove. "I already made the noodles. They're in the fridge. Didn't you hear me say that before I left?"

The misunderstanding grew from there. He expected me to be appreciative and thankful he worked on dinner, which, truth be told, I should have been. I, on the other hand, felt hurt he hadn't listened to me. It wasn't the noodles that bothered me. I felt unheard and ignored.

Thankfully, we were able to move past this disagreement. It's possible we moved past it quickly because we've been married ten years and have finally learned how to let things go. Or it could have been because it wasn't a large dispute anyway. More likely, though, I think the reason we were able to move past the disagreement quickly was because we knew the other person well enough to know they meant well. I knew my husband loved me, so I didn't doubt his love even when his actions could have led me to believe otherwise. Likewise, he knew I loved him, even when I wasn't acting very loving. The reason we were able to move forward was because we both chose to trust the intentions of the other.

I wonder, though, if I'm as trusting of God's intentions when He seems to let me down. When God allows something painful into my life, do I trust Him, or do I question His love for me?

Job is one biblical figure who set an example for us to follow of someone who trusted God's intentions through excruciating circumstances. I've often wondered how he was able to maintain his relationship with God after all he went through. How did Job lose his children, health, and livelihood and still follow the God who was in charge of it all?

God even began the conversation with Satan that started the whole mess. "Have you considered my servant Job?" God asked Satan in Job 1:8. God, not Satan, opened the door for the conversation that devastated Job's life. Then, to make matters worse, God never even told Job why. When Job cried for an explanation, God didn't provide one. Others might have turned their backs on God after this, but not Job.

The more I've thought about this, the more I am convinced he was able to do it because he knew God well enough to know He loved him. Job trusted God's intentions because he knew God's heart.

In Job 1:5, the text says Job's regular custom was offering sacrifices to the Lord. Prayer was his regular custom. It wasn't something he did occasionally, like many of us do today, or something he did when he had enough time or after he finished everything else on his to-do list. It was something he did early in the morning on a regular basis. That custom — which over the years built a relationship between he and the Lord — helped Job know he could count on God even when his life fell apart. Job knew God well enough to know He was worthy of trust.

Even more than that, Job knew God well enough to know He was worthy of praise. In Job 1:21, after Job lost his children, livelihood, and servants, he said, "The LORD gave and the LORD has taken away; may the name of the LORD be praised."

Our God deserves our praise, even when we don't understand

His actions. If there's one thing we can learn from Job, this is it. Even though Job lost everything else, he didn't lose his faith… because faith is something no one — not even Satan — can steal away from us.

When we're in the middle of a painful season, Satan tries to convince us God isn't trustworthy… that He doesn't love us or won't take care of us. Don't believe the lie. God is trustworthy. God is for you. And God is going to work even this for your good.

QUESTIONS FOR REFLECTION

1. Other than Job's prayer life, what do you think helped him maintain his faith through his trials?
2. What things have helped you through your own difficulties?
3. Why is it so difficult to praise God after a tragedy?

PRAYER

Ask God to help you have faith like Job — faith that can stand firm through even the most difficult of circumstances.

SCRIPTURES FOR FURTHER MEDITATION

Habakkuk 3:17–18, Psalm 145:3, Hebrews 10:23, Psalm 46:10

JOURNAL ACTIVITY

Copy Job 1:21 into your journal, then consider committing yourself to praise God, regardless of the outcome of your current situation. After all, He is worthy of praise, even if He doesn't do exactly what we want Him to do.

TAKEAWAY

When difficulties come, choose to trust in
what you know to be true about God.

Peter

Scripture reading: Matthew 14:22–33

"Then Peter got down out of the boat, walked on the water and came toward Jesus. But when he saw the wind, he was afraid and, beginning to sink, cried out, 'Lord, save me!' Immediately Jesus reached out his hand and caught him." — Matthew 14:29–31

One of my favorite things to do is go to my local YMCA. It's not because I'm super-fit or because I love to exercise. Rather, as a stay-at-home mother, it's because sometimes going to the Y is my only "me time." Childcare is provided, so I'm able to take a book with me and read as I use the cycle or elliptical. There are few things I enjoy more than reading. Plus, as an extra bonus, I'm burning calories and getting healthier.

A few months ago, as I headed to the gym early one morning, the sun seemed especially bright. I put on my sunglasses and lowered my visor but still wasn't able to see the road clearly. The sun blurred my vision and blocked the road that was only a few feet in front of me.

Has that ever happened to you? The sun is no brighter in the morning than it is later in the day, but in the morning, the rays are shining directly in your face so you can't see anything else.

Our trials can be a lot like the early morning sun. They become so huge to us they block our vision. They make us unable to see Jesus… even when He's standing right in front of us.

When Peter walked on water, he did something no one else — except for Jesus — had ever done. He had the courage to step out of the boat and into the water. Unfortunately, he failed to maintain that courage because his fears blocked his vision.

I'm getting ahead of myself, though. Let's back up and explore what happened at the beginning of Matthew 14. The chapter opens with a description of John the Baptist's death. After John's disciples buried the body, they came and told Jesus what happened. Then, even though Jesus wanted to be alone to grieve, the crowds followed Him.

When Jesus saw the crowds, He loved them and had compassion on them. Instead of sending them away, Jesus stayed with them the rest of the day. As evening approached, Jesus performed one of His most famous miracles: the feeding of the five thousand with two fish and five loaves of bread. The disciples picked up twelve basketfuls of leftovers and then got into a boat to head to the other side of the lake.

Meanwhile, after Jesus dismissed the crowds and spent time with His heavenly Father, He walked out to the disciples *on* the water. Even though the disciples saw an amazing miracle just hours earlier, they were afraid when Jesus walked toward them. They thought for sure they were seeing a ghost.

Jesus reassured them it was He. "'Lord, if it is you,' Peter replied, 'tell me to come to you on the water.'" (Matt. 14:28) Peter took one step out of the boat, then two, then three. Before he had time to think about what he was doing, Peter walked on water toward Jesus, doing something only he and the Savior of the world had ever done or ever would do.

Peter gets a lot of flack for being impulsive, but he deserves some credit for getting out of the boat. None of the other disciples even took one step. Peter did! Unfortunately, Peter's faith didn't last long enough. The text says when Peter saw the wind, he was afraid. (Matt. 14:30) Peter had faith to walk on water when his eyes were focused on Jesus, but the moment he took his eyes off his Savior and put them on the storm around him, he began to sink.

Friend, I don't know what storm threatens you today. But I do know focusing on the storm isn't going to help. Focus instead on Jesus, the One who is able to calm the storm… or, at the very least, calm His child within the storm.

The best way I have found to do this is to pay attention to your thoughts. When you realize you're focusing exclusively on your problem, change your focus by thinking about something else. Grab your Bible and read from it. Read some of the Scriptures for Further Meditation listed below.

Replace your fearful thoughts with prayers. List some things for which you are thankful. Our thoughts dictate our focus, so the best way to change our focus is to change our thoughts.

When the sun blocked my vision on the way to the gym, the only way I was able to see again was to stop looking directly into the light. To take my eyes off the sun and look away. Today, can I challenge you to do the same: take your eyes off your current situation and look away? Better yet, look toward Jesus, who, as Hebrews 12:2 says is "the pioneer and perfecter of faith."

QUESTIONS FOR REFLECTION

1. What trial threatens to block your vision of Jesus right now?
2. What can you do to fix your eyes on Jesus, rather than your storm?

PRAYER

Pray for eyes that focus on Jesus instead of on problems. Ask the Lord to help you do this throughout the day.

SCRIPTURES FOR FURTHER MEDITATION

Hebrews 12:1–3, Proverbs 4:25–27, Colossians 3:2

JOURNAL ACTIVITY

Write the following verses in your journal: "Let us run with perseverance the race marked out for us, fixing our eyes on Jesus, the pioneer and perfecter of faith." (Heb. 12:1–2) Then write one specific thing you plan to do this week to help you fix your eyes on Jesus.

TAKEAWAY

When difficulties come, fix your eyes on Jesus, not on the storm.

Paul and Silas

Scripture reading: Acts 16:16–34

"After they had been severely flogged, they were thrown into prison, and the jailer was commanded to guard them carefully. When he received these orders, he put them in the inner cell and fastened their feet in the stocks. About midnight Paul and Silas were praying and singing hymns to God, and the other prisoners were listening to them." — Acts 16:23–25

On November 17, 2012, after we lost our fourth baby to miscarriage, I wrote this blog post:

Nine weeks, two days. This pregnancy, just like several of our other ones, only lasted nine weeks and two days.

Last week, we saw and heard a great heartbeat. One hundred fifty-nine to be exact. Strong enough I thought maybe, just maybe, this time was going to be different. It wasn't.

Our doctor was quiet when he started the ultrasound. He looked around for what felt like hours and still didn't say a word. "Is there a heartbeat?" I finally broke the silence.

He looked at me with kindness in his eyes. "I'm so sorry."

Now we grieve again. I didn't want to go through this. I wanted this time to be different. I wanted to bring home a baby from the hospital. Not just another ultrasound picture. My son wanted a little sister. I wanted a daughter. As it looks now, neither one of us will ever get our wish.

Last Sunday at church, before this doctor's appointment, we sang "Desert Song" by Hillsong. This song was hard for me with our other miscarriages, so it was an emotional song already. As we sang it on Sunday (well, as everyone else sang and I cried), I told God I would trust him regardless of what happened with this pregnancy, regardless of the results of this appointment.

I stand by that promise today. I will choose to say, blessed be the name of the Lord, even when it hurts.

It's great to worship God when life goes well, but can we do it when He doesn't answer our prayers as we expect Him to? Can we still worship Him when life isn't working out as we planned?

Paul and Silas could. In Acts 16, as they traveled from town to town sharing about Jesus, they met a slave girl possessed by an evil spirit that enabled her to tell the future. This girl followed Paul and Silas around for days, shouting to anyone who would listen, "These men are servants of the Most High God, who are telling you the way to be saved." (Acts 16:17) Finally, Paul had enough of it. After all, who wants an evil spirit providing an endorsement? Paul commanded the spirit to leave the girl, and the spirit obeyed.

You'd think the girl's owners would be happy an evil spirit left their servant. Instead, all they thought about was the money they were now going to lose because she couldn't tell the future anymore. They dragged Paul and Silas into the marketplace and created such an uproar that Paul and Silas were stripped, beaten with rods, and thrown into prison.

After this happened, even while their feet were secured in the stocks, Paul and Silas prayed and sang hymns to God. (Acts 16:25) Picture this scene with me. Two men who have just been severely flogged, who still have blood seeping from their fresh wounds, who can barely stand because of the pain, sing to the Lord in worship. That is commitment. That is faith. And that is what I'm challenging each of us to do today.

When difficulties come your way, you might be tempted to stop attending church. You might be tempted to stop singing to the One who chose not to save you from your struggle. Believe me, I've been there. There have been many Sundays I've wondered, Why am I still going? Why do I continue to pray when God doesn't seem to listen?

You might wonder similar things — if you should give up on God or if you're better off going your own way. Please don't do it. Please choose to worship anyway.

Worship God, not because of what He has or has not done for you, but because of who He is. He is our Redeemer. He is our Savior. He is the First and the Last. He is the One who gave His life for us. Worship Him for who He is, not for what He can give you.

Have you ever witnessed someone worshiping through pain? A

friend of mine lost her baby a few months ago. Days after the funeral, I watched her lift her hands to the Lord in worship. It was one of the most beautiful — and heartbreaking — things I have ever seen. It was also a testimony to everyone around her. Her God was still worthy of worship, even when He didn't fix her problems.

I imagine that's exactly what the people in jail with Paul and Silas thought too. Some of them might have even chosen to sing right along with them in prison. One thing is certain: when we choose to worship God with broken hearts, the world takes note.

QUESTIONS FOR REFLECTION

1. When is it hardest for you to worship?
2. Will you choose to worship God today, regardless of your circumstances? If you're willing and able, find one of your favorite worship songs on YouTube and worship right now.

PRAYER

Pray for God to help you worship Him, even when it hurts. Ask Him to fill your heart with love and admiration for who He is.

SCRIPTURES FOR FURTHER MEDITATION

Hebrews 10:24–25, 32–5, James 1:2–4, Psalm 33:1–22

JOURNAL ACTIVITY

List all of the characteristics of God that make Him worthy of praise

TAKEAWAY

When difficulties come, praise God anyway.

When God Is Nowhere to Be Found

W here are you, God?"

Most of us have, at one point or another, asked this question. We've wondered how this (whatever this is) could be happening if God were really near.

In the pages of God's Word are examples of others who asked similar questions. For instance, in Psalm 88, the sons of Asaph asked God, "Why, LORD, do you… hide your face from me?" (Ps. 88:14)

This week, we'll look at five examples of people from the Bible who had good reason to wonder where God went. We'll study the lives of Esther and Elisha's servant. We'll look at Jesus' disciples. We'll also study two separate instances when the Israelites could have easily felt as though God had left them.

Each of these stories will remind us that just because God doesn't appear to be with us doesn't mean He's gone. Sometimes, as you'll see in the pages ahead, God's apparent absence means He's working behind the scenes and getting ready to show up in indescribable ways.

After you complete this week's lessons, please watch the video at…

www.crossrivermedia.com/portfolio/unbeaten-week-two

Esther

Scripture reading: Esther 4:5–14

*"And who knows but that you have come to your royal
position for such a time as this?" — Esther 4:14*

W hat's your name, Mommy?" my two-year-old son asked
me as I pushed him in the swing in our backyard. Earlier that day, I taught him his full name, so I assume
that's what brought on the question. He knew Daddy's name was Keith
Bell, he knew Bubby's name, and now he knew his own name, but he
wasn't sure about mine.

"What do you think my name is?" I asked him.

He looked at me with his big blue eyes. "Mommy Bell?"

There's just something about hearing your name, isn't there, especially when it's coming from the mouth of a child you adore? I remember the first time my oldest son said "Mommy." It too had melted my
heart and made me wish I could stop time at that very moment.

When my husband and I said goodbye to the babies we had hoped
to raise, we named each of them: Eden, Jesse, Ella, and Jadon. We didn't
have to name them, because there was no death certificate since they died
inside the womb. Still, naming them comforted my heart in some strange
way. I knew they were real, but when I named them, I told the rest of the
world, "These are my kids! They matter! Their lives were short, but they
still existed." It was almost as if giving them a name gave them a place
within our family. I didn't just have a miscarriage; I lost Eden. I didn't just
lose a baby; I lost my baby. The difference might seem miniscule on paper,
but in my heart it was huge. The names made all the difference.

Because of how important names are — both today and in biblical
times — it seems odd God's name is never mentioned in the book of

Esther. His name is absent from the entire book, not mentioned even one time. How could a book of the Bible, the very words of God, miss His name in its pages? And if His name isn't in it, was He still there?

To make matters worse, Esther's difficult life certainly didn't appear to have God's hands on it. And honestly, difficult doesn't even begin to describe Esther's circumstances. She had the kind of life little girls dread. She became an orphan at a young age when both of her parents died. Her uncle stepped in to raise her, but then, in her teen years, the pagan king forced her to come to him for no other reason than sex. After sleeping with her, the king then decided whether or not he liked her enough to keep her around.

Esther had good reason to doubt God's presence in her life. What's amazing is that even though God's presence might not have been felt, His fingerprints were all over this story. They showed up when a pagan man elected Esther, an Israelite, queen. They showed up again when that pagan king couldn't sleep one night and chose to read history books. What page do you suppose God led the king to read? He led the king to the page that told about Mordecai, Esther's Jewish uncle, saving the king from an assassination plot years earlier. God's fingerprints showed up when Haman plotted for the destruction of the Jews at the exact same time the king wanted to honor a Jew.

The name of God is never mentioned in the book of Esther, but His fingerprints are all over the book. When Esther learned about Haman's plot to destroy her people, her uncle Mordecai said the famous words that began today's devotional. Esther became queen at "such a time as this" because God was working behind the scenes to save His people. It was not coincidental how Esther's life unfolded. Rather, it was God, working out the circumstances of her life and bringing her to this very moment — the moment she saved an entire nation of people.

Today, if you doubt God's presence in your life or if you wonder why you can't see or feel Him anymore, take a lesson from the book of Esther. Just because you can't see God doesn't mean He's not there.

Maybe, as in the case with Esther, His fingerprints are all over you. And maybe you can't see His name in your story because He's written it on your forehead. In Revelation 22:4, John wrote, "They will see his face, and his name will be on their foreheads." Take a look in the mirror. Is it possible God's name is written there? You might not see God's handiwork in your life yet, but in time I bet the letters will begin to show through.

QUESTIONS FOR REFLECTION

1. What situation in your life has made you feel as though God is no longer with you?
2. What are some ways God's fingerprints have left their mark on your current situation?
3. What's the significance of a name?

PRAYER

Pray for eyes to see God's activity in your day-to-day life. Ask God to reveal His fingerprints, especially in those moments when you begin to doubt His presence.

SCRIPTURES FOR FURTHER MEDITATION

Hebrews 13:2, 1 Kings 19:11–13, Revelation 22:4

JOURNAL ACTIVITY

What does your name mean? Write it in your journal. Then, look up the following verses and write in your journal some of the other names God gave you through His Word: Ephesians 2:10, 1 John 3:1, Psalm 139:14, Genesis 1:27

TAKEAWAY

When you can't find God, look for His fingerprints.

DAY TWO

The Israelites in Egypt

Scripture reading: Genesis 15:13–14

"Then the LORD said to him, 'Know for certain that for four hundred years your descendants will be strangers in a country not their own and that they will be enslaved and mistreated there." — Genesis 15:13

Have you ever prayed for something over and over again? Has one thing been on your prayer list for not just days, but also years? Maybe it's for a husband or for a child. Maybe it's for the restoration of a relationship or for a job. Whatever it is, it might be causing you to look into the sky and ask God something like this:

When, God? When are you going to move? Haven't I waited long enough?

Maybe you've asked, as the psalmist did in Psalm 10:1, "Why, LORD, do you stand far off? Why do you hide yourself in times of trouble?"

I imagine the Israelites prayed similar words many times as they suffered in Egypt. In a later devotional, we're going to look in depth at the life of Joseph. His story, though, begins here. At the end of his life, after going through more than any one person should ever endure, God finally redeemed all the years Joseph lost. He freed him from prison, restored the relationships in his family, and made Joseph famous throughout the land of Egypt.

Years passed, though, and eventually Joseph died and the people forgot all about the things he did for Egypt and the surrounding nations. Here's what the text says, "Then a new king, to whom Joseph meant nothing, came to power in Egypt. 'Look,' he said to his people, 'the Israelites have become far too numerous for us. Come, we must deal shrewdly with them or they will become even more numerous

33

and, if war breaks out, will join our enemies, fight against us and leave the country.'" (Exodus 1:8-10)

This new king feared the Israelites so much he forced them into servitude. Worse yet, he ordered the midwives to kill all the Hebrew boys when they were born. These were the conditions the Lord predicted in Genesis 15, our text for today.

There is one thing you need to understand about this servitude. We shouldn't simply imagine difficult labor, though it was certainly that. Instead, as the text says, we should imagine oppressive and ruthless conditions (Exodus 1:13-14). The Egyptians made the Israelites' lives "bitter with harsh labor." One commentary I read even said the Egyptians were "specialists at making a slave's life miserable."[1]

When I think of a specialist, I picture someone in the medical field: a heart specialist, cancer specialist, or specialist of pediatric medicine. What I don't think of is someone who specializes in torture, cruelty, and fear.

To make matters worse, this torture went on for decades. Scratch that. It went on for centuries. Four hundred years, to be exact. God allowed the Israelites to remain in servitude to the Egyptians for 400 years. That is 400 years of prayers, 400 years of wondering if and when God would come to their rescue, and 400 years of doubting whether He still cared about His people.

That, my friends, is a *long* time to wait for God to answer a prayer. Many of the Israelites died without His answer. Quite possibly, they died wondering if He heard their cries of distress and wondering why — if He heard them — He failed to do anything about it.

It might be tempting to think God didn't care about their suffering, just as it might be tempting to think He doesn't care about ours. The truth is, God does care. He cared then, and He cares now.

In Exodus 3, when God called Moses to lead the Israelites out of Egypt, here is what He said. "I have indeed seen the misery of my people in Egypt. I have heard them crying out because of their slave drivers, and I am concerned about their suffering." (Exodus 3:7)

If God were in your room right now, sitting beside you as you read this book, I think He might say the same thing to you: "I have seen your misery, I have heard you crying out, and I am concerned about you." God might not have answered your prayer yet, or He might not have answered it in a way you wanted Him to, but know this: He does care about what's going on in your life. He is not now — and never will be — oblivious to your suffering.

QUESTIONS FOR REFLECTION

1. Why do you think God waited 400 years before He stepped in and freed the Israelites? There is no right or wrong answer, so take as many guesses as you'd like.

2. What is something that has been on your prayer list for a while? Can you think of any possible reason God hasn't come to your rescue yet?

PRAYER

Pray for patience as you wait for an answer from the Lord. Ask Him to remind you on the hard days that He has heard you, seen you, and loved you.

SCRIPTURES FOR FURTHER MEDITATION

Psalm 10:1, Hebrews 11:13–16, Psalm 34:15, 17–18

JOURNAL ACTIVITY

In your journal, list your prayer requests. Beside the list, write these words, "God sees. God hears. God cares." Then read Psalm 13 and underline any part of this Psalm that speaks to your current situation. If any verses encourage you, write them in your journal.

TAKEAWAY

When you can't find God, know He has heard you,
seen you, and cares deeply about you.

Elisha's Servant

Scripture reading: 2 Kings 6:8–17

*"Don't be afraid," the prophet answered.
"Those who are with us are more than those
who are with them." And Elisha prayed, "Open his
eyes, LORD, so that he may see." — 2 Kings 6:16–17*

n Jennifer Rothschild's book *God is Just Not Fair*, she tells the story of a woman named Susan who lost her sight at age thirty-three.[2] When Susan first lost her ability to see, she struggled to complete even the simplest tasks like cooking, cleaning, and getting showered for the day.

Eventually, though, Susan learned how to function again. She learned how to put her makeup on, how to cook, and even how to go to work. When she first went back to work, her husband drove her. Unfortunately, this made it impossible for him to make it to work on time. He tried numerous routes through the city, but none were successful. Finally, he told Susan she needed to ride the bus to work.

To prepare her for the task, Mark rode the bus with her for several weeks. He introduced her to the bus driver and helped her get accustomed to the route. When the day finally came for Susan to ride the bus by herself, she was nervous, of course, but everything went smoothly.

At the end of the week, the bus driver said something to Susan that confused her. He told her she must feel good about herself because she was so well cared for. After a week of riding a bus by herself, as a blind woman, no less, she had no idea what he was talking about. She questioned him, "Are you talking to me?" He reassured her he was and then told her about her hidden hero, the man down the street who watched to make sure she made it to work okay.

Susan didn't know her husband Mark hadn't let her ride the bus completely by herself yet. As far as she knew, he was on his way to work. What she failed to see was that he had watched her from a distance every step of the way. When the bus stopped at her office, he stood on the corner and kept his eyes glued to her. He watched her slowly get off the bus and cautiously walk toward the door. He watched her hand reach for the doorknob. Then, once he knew she was safely inside, he saluted her and went to work himself.

Susan thought she was alone, but she wasn't. Sometimes it's the same with us. We think we're alone and that God is no longer with us, but our sight is not the best indicator of reality. Just as Susan couldn't see her husband standing down the street from her, we can't always see God… even when He is just around the corner from us. Sight isn't always the best sign of what's really there.

Take a look at the prophet Elisha's servant in 2 Kings 6, for example. The Aramean army surrounded Elisha's town and planned to capture him for helping the Israelite army. When Elisha's servant saw the army surrounding the city, he cried to Elisha, "Oh no, my lord! What shall we do?" (2 Kings 6:15)

Elisha prayed for the Lord to open the servant's eyes. When the servant looked around again, he saw horses and chariots of fire on the hills all around Elisha. (2 Kings 6:17) What Elisha's servant hadn't realized, and what we often forget, is that what's in front of us isn't everything there is to see. Sometimes, things are going on our eyes can't see.

Another biblical example of this is in Daniel 10. When Daniel prayed for understanding, a man came to him and said, "*Since the first day* that you set your mind to gain understanding… your words were heard, and I have come in response to them. But the prince of the Persian kingdom resisted me twenty-one days. Then Michael, one of the chief princes, came to help me, because I was detained there with the king of Persia." (Daniel 10:12-13, emphasis mine) Did you catch the first part of this verse? God heard Daniel's prayer on *the first day* he called out. The messenger, though, was held back for twenty-one days because of a battle Daniel wasn't able to see.

Is it possible something is going on in our situations we're not able to see? Is it possible God is working behind the scenes to answer our prayers? Is it possible our sight isn't the only reality there is? That maybe, just maybe, it's the things we can't see — the One we can't see — that makes all the difference in the world.

QUESTIONS FOR REFLECTION

1. Why do you think it's difficult to focus on what we can't see?
2. Read over the questions in the last paragraph again. Thinking about your situation (and being completely honest with yourself), do you think it's possible there is more going on than you can see?

PRAYER

Pray God opens your eyes to some of the things that are unseen. Ask Him to show you His presence, especially in those moments when He feels far from you.

SCRIPTURES FOR FURTHER MEDITATION

2 Corinthians 4:18, Hebrews 11:1,
Daniel 10 (especially verses 12 and 13)

JOURNAL ACTIVITY

Copy 2 Corinthians 4:18 in your journal: "So we fix our eyes not on what is seen, but on what is unseen, since what is seen is temporary, but what is unseen is eternal."

TAKEAWAY

When you can't find God, remember there is
more going on around us than our earthly eyes can see.

The Israelites Between the Testaments

Scripture reading: Galatians 4:4 and Matthew 1:18–25

"But when the set time had fully come, God sent his Son, born of a woman, born under the law." — Galatians 4:4

My two boys love to play hide and seek. When I played as a child, I remember getting knots in my stomach as my excitement grew. Were they going to find me? Did I hide well enough? Where are they now?

The first time I played with my kids, I assumed those knots were long gone. What adult gets excited playing hide and seek with two kids under five? I was surprised when I felt that same surge of excitement hiding behind my couch. My breathing grew more rapid and my stomach churned with excitement as I waited for my children to walk around the corner and spot me in my admittedly bad hiding place.

Hide and seek is fun when you want to play, but what happens when only one person wants to play? Like when your child hides from you but somehow forgets to invite you to join? When hide and seek is one-sided, the fun dissipates and worry sets in.

My youngest son once did this, and I almost called the police. Thankfully, he made a noise, and I was able to find him. Hide and seek stops being fun when you can't find the missing person.

Have you ever felt like God was hiding from you? As I mentioned in the introduction to this week's topic, the sons of Asaph asked God in Psalm 88:14, "Why, LORD, do you... hide your face from me?" When God seems to be hiding His face from you and when you search for Him and can't find Him, the pain and anxiety that follows can be excruciating.

I think the Israelites probably went through a time when they wondered where God was hiding from them. A couple of days ago, we studied the Israelites of the Old Testament. We looked at what life was like for them in Egypt. Many of these men and women probably questioned where God was during those 400 years of torture.

A little while later, there was another 400 years to note. These 400 years took place between the Old and New Testaments. During that time, not one word came from the Father. No one added any more inspired words to the Bible. No prophets spoke words from God. It was completely silent for 400 years. As far as the Israelites were concerned, God was nowhere to be found. Just as the Israelites in Egypt probably felt unheard, these Israelites might have felt abandoned too.

Can you imagine how frustrated they must have become? Was God ever going to fulfill all the things He promised through His prophets? Would He ever send a Savior? Where was He?

Hindsight, of course, is 20/20, so we're able to understand some things now they might not have understood then. For instance, we now know there were a lot of things that happened during those 400 years that prepared the way for Jesus' coming. The Roman Empire unified the world in such a way that travel was easier than it had ever been before, thus opening the door for believers to share the gospel. Another reason sharing the gospel was possible after this time was because there was a common language.

God sent His Son, according to Galatians 4, "when the set time had fully come." He might not have been talking a whole lot in those 400 years between the testaments, but He wasn't taking a nap either. He was busy making sure the world was just as He wanted it before His Son came.

Have you ever thought about the name God gave Jesus when he was born? He gave him the name "Immanuel (which means 'God with us')." (Matthew 1:23) I love that! After 400 years of silence, God proved He never left. He was — and is — God with us!

I'm not sure why He sometimes seems hidden, just as the Israelites probably didn't understand why God seemed hidden from them in the time period between the testaments. The thing to keep in mind is, someday, on this side of heaven or the other, hindsight will be 20/20. It will all make sense… someday.

On that day, some of us will discover God wasn't really hiding His face from us. Instead, He was busy preparing us for something in our futures. In God's kingdom, times of waiting are never wasted. The question is, are we letting our wait go to waste, or are we allowing God to use it for His glory?

One thing I've noticed as I play hide and seek with my children is that they make noise to be found. If I'm taking too long searching for them, they start yelling for me or moving around or knocking on doors or walls. They don't want to stay hidden forever, so they make noise to be found.

If you feel stuck in an unwanted game of hide and seek with God, start making noise. Cry out to Him, and ask Him to come to you. He is the God who sees (Genesis 16:13). He'll come find you soon.

QUESTIONS FOR REFLECTION

1. What do you think went through the Israelites' minds during the time between the testaments?
2. Do you think it possible God is preparing you for something through your time of waiting? Why or why not?

PRAYER

Pray God would grow your patience as you wait for Him to move in your life. Pray He would use times of waiting for His glory and your strengthening.

SCRIPTURES FOR FURTHER MEDITATION

Matthew 1, Psalm 13

JOURNAL ACTIVITY

What are some things you can do in this time of waiting? As you wait for God to show up, what can you do to make sure you are ready for Him? Write down any ideas that come to mind. For instance, you could try to read your Bible every day. Or you could commit to praying first thing in the morning, even before you check your phone or get ready for the day.

TAKEAWAY

When you can't find God, remember He might be
working behind the scenes, preparing you for your future.

Jesus' Disciples

Scripture reading: Mark 16:1–14

*"You are looking for Jesus the Nazarene,
who was crucified. He has risen! He is not here.
See the place where they laid him." — Mark 16:6*

Maybe you've heard about Tony Campolo's famous sermon called "It's Friday but Sunday's Coming." The words in that title have become popular among Christians. You might be in a tough spot right now, they say, but Sunday's coming! Basically, what they are saying is, just as Jesus' death on Friday was dark for the disciples, your life might be dark right now. But hang on. The disciples didn't see Jesus' resurrection coming, just like you might not be able to fathom what God is getting ready to do in your life. It might be Friday or Saturday in your life now, friends, but Sunday's heading your way.

About a month after our third miscarriage, I sank into what I now assume was depression. I was still able to function and had to for my son, but I felt stuck in my grief. I was stuck in Saturday.

Then, late one evening, my mom called and asked if we could Skype with her. This might be a normal occurrence for some people, but not for us. This was far from ordinary, so my mind wandered to who-knows-how-many possible situations. Did someone die? Did Dad lose his job? Are you moving? Why in the world does Mom want to Skype?

The one thing I didn't assume was that God was preparing me for my Sunday. In the Skype conversation with my mom, she asked if my husband and I would be interested in adopting a baby boy who was due in two months. Keep in mind, we weren't seeking to adopt. We didn't even know how to adopt. We had no home study, no paperwork, and no attorney... and only two months before the baby would be born.

As I disconnected the call, my entire body shook with the tears I had been holding in for so long. Could we really get a baby in two months?

We tried to keep our emotions out of it, just in case the birthparents changed their minds, but as each day passed, I grew more and more excited. God hadn't forgotten me, and my Sunday — my day of redemption — was coming soon. I was convinced of it.

Two months after that Skype call, I cut the umbilical cord of our new baby boy. Tears blinded my vision as I held him in my arms and rocked him back and forth in a quiet hospital room. Our new baby didn't replace the ones we had lost, but he did remind me Saturdays don't last forever. In God's Kingdom, Sunday is always coming.

We later learned why our son's birth mom chose us. When she decided at seven months pregnant she wanted to choose adoption, she asked two different people whom they thought she should choose as parents. Both of these people, unbeknownst to each other, said us. The reason they picked us was because of our miscarriages and how much they knew we longed for a baby. The very thing that broke me — our miscarriages — was also the very thing God used to bring a baby into our home.

My Friday was dark, my Saturday even darker, but when Sunday finally came, it was brighter than I could have imagined. God hadn't left me on Saturday, and He hasn't left you either.[3]

As I've thought about this topic, God keeps bringing me back to Jesus' disciples. On Friday, Jesus died on a wooden cross. His disciples had previously thought He was the Savior of the world. They placed all their hopes and dreams in Him. But then, He died, and dying with Him were their dreams for a future.

On Saturday, Jesus lay dead in a tomb, and His disciples quivered in hiding. They probably wondered what they would do next. Could they really go back to their jobs, as if nothing had changed? How could they go on living when the One who claimed to be the Life was dead?

Friday was dark for the disciples, but Saturday might have been even darker, because it was the day reality set in. There would be no more walks beside the sea with their Lord. There would be no more miracles. No more parables. No more salvation. Everything they hoped for in the past three years was now buried in the tomb with Jesus' decaying body.

But then Sunday came. That day changed everything. It changed everything for the disciples, but it also changed everything for you and me.

Because Sunday came for Jesus and His disciples, we can *know*, not just wish, our Sundays are coming too. They might come on this side of heaven or they might come on the other side of heaven, but they are coming. Sunday is heading your way, so keep your eyes peeled for it.

QUESTIONS FOR REFLECTION

1. Read through all four accounts of the resurrection (Matthew 28:1-7; Mark 16:1-8; Luke 24:1-12; John 20:1-9.) What do you think the women felt as they headed toward the tomb that morning? What about when they headed away from it?
2. What emotions do you think the disciples felt on Saturday?

PRAYER

Pray for your Sunday. Ask God to help you as you go through Friday and Saturday, and ask Him to bring Sunday soon.

SCRIPTURES FOR FURTHER MEDITATION

James 1:12, 2 Timothy 3:12, John 16:16-22

JOURNAL ACTIVITY

Make three columns in your journal and label them: Friday, Saturday, Sunday. Under each heading, list some of the emotions the disciples probably felt on each day. Make another column below this one with the same headings. Then put an X where you think you are right now. Pray for Sunday to come soon.

TAKEAWAY

When you can't find God, keep your eyes peeled for Sunday.

When God Seems Late

There's a quote by Dillon Burroughs that says, "God is never late and rarely early. He is exactly right on time — His time."[1] I love the sentiment behind this quote, but at times I struggle with it because of my circumstances. It *feels* like God is late sometimes.

When the money runs out…

When a loved one dies…

When the healing doesn't come…

When a car accident steals a life too soon…

In these moments, even though I know in my head God's timing is perfect, my heart doesn't agree. It feels like God is late. This week, we're going to look at this topic and examine the lives of several biblical figures who could have easily thought God wasn't on time.

Mary and Martha, as well as Jairus, watched their loved ones die because Jesus didn't make it to their towns in time to save them. Stephen also tasted death because God didn't show up in time. Hannah, Abram, and Sarai each battled with God over His apparent lack of urgency. Each of these men and women answered the question we often ask: what do you do when God seems slow in responding to your prayers?

After you complete this week's lessons, please watch the video at…

www.crossrivermedia.com/portfolio/unbeaten-week-three

Mary, Martha, and Lazarus

Scripture reading: John 11:1–44

"When Mary reached the place where Jesus was and saw him, she fell at his feet and said, 'Lord, if you had been here, my brother would not have died.'" — John 11:32

Mary's words sound familiar to me, probably because I've said similar ones numerous times in the last few years. *Lord, if you had been here, my babies wouldn't have died.* I believed, just as Mary did, Jesus was capable of changing the future. He was capable of doing a miracle, but for whatever reason, chose not to.

Maybe you've said similar words too:

Lord, if you had been here, my husband would not have left me.

God, if you had been here, I wouldn't have lost my job.

Lord, if you had been here, my child wouldn't have died.

Mary, Martha, and Lazarus were some of Jesus' closest friends. Even still, when Lazarus became ill and Mary and Martha sent for Jesus, He "stayed where he was two more days." (John 11:6) Why the delay?

If Jesus loved them, and the text says He does, why didn't He come immediately? I think the same question could be asked in regard to us. If Jesus loves us, and again, the Bible makes it abundantly clear He does, why doesn't He always come to our aid immediately when we call to Him? Why are there times it seems He keeps His distance when we need Him most?

I can't help but wonder if maybe Jesus doesn't come to us immediately for the same reason He didn't come to Mary and Martha: because He wants us to see His glory. In John 11:40, after Lazarus died and Jesus finally did come to Mary and Martha, He said to them, "Did I not tell you that if you believe, you will see the glory of God?" With those words, Jesus raised Lazarus from the dead.

So maybe, just maybe, God is preparing to do something amazing in your life that can only be done if He allows whatever difficulty you are facing at this moment. Maybe it's precisely because of the difficulty He is able to do this amazing thing.

That is what happened with my husband and me. Our miscarriages were the avenue God used to bring us a baby. It was because of them, our son's birthmother even considered us. In essence, our miscarriages paved the way for our adoption.

Without the losses, we wouldn't have the gain. If God had shown up on my time and saved the babies we lost, we wouldn't have our son.

Because of our limited vantage point, we struggle to see how painful things can be part of God's plan. It reminds me of the disciples before Jesus' death. In Matthew 16:22, when Jesus told them what was about to happen, Peter challenged Jesus. "'Never, Lord!' he said. 'This shall never happen to you!'" Jesus turned to Peter and rebuked him. "You do not have in mind the concerns of God, but merely human concerns."

It's easy to get caught up in this world and in the problems we face today, just as easy as it was for Jesus' disciples and for Mary and Martha. We see what's right in front of us, not what the future holds. Unfortunately, when we do this, we risk missing the glory of God. Maybe when God seems late, He's not really late. Maybe instead, He's getting ready to reveal His glory.

In the Hall of Faith chapter in Hebrews, there are a couple of verses I find interesting: Hebrews 11:39-40. After describing several of the heroes of the faith, the author wrote, "These were all commended for their faith, yet none of them received what had been promised, since God had planned something better for us so that only together with us would they be made perfect."

Each of the men and women listed in Hebrews 11 had faith God would do something amazing. None of them, however, were alive to witness that amazing thing actually come to pass.

Here's the takeaway. God's promises *always* come true. He is *always* faithful. It might not look like it today or even tomorrow. But eventually, when we're able to see the entire timeline of our lives, it will be clear to us.

Just as Mary and Martha had to endure Lazarus' death to witness his resurrection, and just as the people in Hebrews 11 had to wait hundreds of years before they saw God's promises fulfilled, we might have to go through our own dark days before the light finally comes. It will come, though, because we have a God who always keeps His promises.

QUESTIONS FOR REFLECTION

1. Describe a time when God has used something terrible in your life or those you know to bring about something good?
2. What other reasons might have caused Jesus' delay?
3. Do you agree or disagree with the quote by Dillon Burroughs, "God is never late, and rarely early"? Why?

PRAYER

Pray for God to help you trust in His timing. Pray for patience as you wait for His assistance.

SCRIPTURES FOR FURTHER MEDITATION

Matthew 16:21–23, Hebrews 11:39–40, Psalm 119:90

JOURNAL ACTIVITY

Read John 11 in its entirety. What do you think would have happened if Jesus had shown up before Lazarus died? Write a couple of possible scenarios in your journal. Then, draw a picture of a clock as a reminder that God's delays could be for good reason.

TAKEAWAY

When God seems late, continue to wait and watch for His glory.

Stephen

Scripture reading: Acts 6:7–7:60

"But Stephen, full of the Holy Spirit, looked up to heaven and saw the glory of God, and Jesus standing at the right hand of God." — Acts 7:55

Why isn't He helping me? Why isn't He there when I cry out to Him?" Her words came to me over a text message late one evening. Though I couldn't see her, I knew how she probably looked: eyes red from crying, face blotchy from tears, and her beautiful smile gone. My friend wanted to feel God's presence and to know He was with her, but she struggled to sense Him because of what she was going through.

Like the Psalmist, she wondered, "How long, Lᴏʀᴅ? Will you forget me forever? How long will you hide your face from me? How long must I wrestle with my thoughts and day after day have sorrow in my heart?" (Ps. 13:1-2) My heart went out to her because I, too, have felt this way. My guess is, so have you.

As we look at the life of Stephen, or more accurately, as we look at his death, I think we might find an answer to the question of where God is when we need Him.

Stephen was the first Christian martyr. He is first introduced in Acts 6 as a man full of faith and the Holy Spirit. Stephen did many miracles among the people. Unfortunately, he also created quite a stir when he spoke about Jesus. The people brought him before the Sanhedrin, the Jewish religious leaders, and asked him about his beliefs.

Stephen told these leaders how Jesus fulfilled every Old Testament prophecy and promise about the Messiah. He also challenged them for their part in Jesus' death. At this, the religious leaders "gnashed their teeth at him" (Acts 7:54) and refused to listen anymore. If he wouldn't stop speaking, they would silence him, and that is exactly what they did. As they picked up stones to throw, Stephen got a glimpse of glory.

> "But Stephen, full of the Holy Spirit, looked up to heaven and saw the glory of God, and Jesus standing at the right hand of God. 'Look,' he said, 'I see heaven open and the Son of Man standing at the right hand of God.'" (Acts 7:55–56)

There's something unique about this text I want to make sure you catch. Often in Scripture, when Jesus is in heaven with God, He is seated — not standing like in this text. Take a look at Mark 16:19, for example. "After the Lord Jesus had spoken to them, he was taken up to heaven, and he sat at the right hand of God." Other verses, like Ephesians 1:20 and Hebrews 1:3, also describe Jesus as seated.

Why was Jesus standing in Acts? Biblical scholars can't agree. Some believe Jesus stood to show his approval of Stephen and to encourage him. Others believe He stood as a sign of judgment on the religious leaders. Some claim it was because He was standing before God, mediating on behalf of Stephen. There's no way to know for certain, but I love the theory He stood to support and encourage Stephen.

Imagine trading places with Stephen. Maybe you began your speech with confidence, but then, as you watch your enemies pick up stones to heave at you, you start to fear. Maybe you even begin to doubt. Could that be why Jesus stood, so Stephen could see Him easier and so Stephen would know for sure he wasn't alone? Is it possible Jesus stood so Stephen could see Him, instead of his attackers?

As Stephen faced an excruciating death, Jesus didn't remain in His chair. That is powerful to me, whether He did it to encourage Stephen or for one of the other suggested reasons. He didn't just sit there, void of emotion. He rose to His feet so Stephen could see the face of the Man worth dying for. At a moment when many would be tempted to give up their faith, Jesus made certain Stephen knew the sacrifice was worth the cost. He stood to His feet to cheer on His faithful disciple. I imagine if He spoke, He might have said something like this, "You can do this, Stephen. Hang tough. I am with you."

I don't know exactly where Jesus is when we are hurting. I don't know if He's sitting or standing in heaven. But based on what He did when Stephen needed Him most, I'd like to think if we could peek into heaven at those times when we are crying out to Him, we might see Him standing for us too. We might hear Him saying, "You can do this. Hang tough. I am with you."

QUESTIONS FOR REFLECTION

1. Why do you think Jesus stood when Stephen was killed? (There are no right or wrong answers, so use your imagination.)
2. How does it make you feel to think of God cheering for you during difficult times?

PRAYER

Thank your loving Father He cares about your struggles and never takes His eyes off of you. Ask Him to remind you of His attention at times when you begin to doubt.

SCRIPTURES FOR FURTHER MEDITATION

1 Corinthians 10:13, Isaiah 41:10, John 16:33

JOURNAL ACTIVITY

Read Psalm 121. Then write in your journal a few of the verses in that psalm that spoke to your heart.

TAKEAWAY

When God seems late, imagine Jesus standing in heaven, cheering you on.

Hannah

Scripture reading: 1 Samuel 1:1–28

"'I prayed for this child, and the LORD has granted me what I asked of him. So now I give him to the LORD. For his whole life he will be given over to the LORD.' And he worshiped the LORD there." — 1 Samuel 1:27–28

A couple of days ago, my two-year-old son threw one of the biggest fits I have ever seen. Though I wish I could tell you it was because of something important, it wasn't. He was screaming and flailing his little body on the floor because I wouldn't allow him to stand on his chair as he ate his breakfast. He just didn't get to do something he wanted.

It's easy to look at a toddler in the middle of a tantrum and think about the silliness of his or her problem. After all, compared to the sometimes larger-than-life problems many adults face, an unmet desire isn't really that big of a deal.

If you think about it, though, a two-year-old throws a fit for pretty much the same reason an adult might throw her own adult version. Our tantrums might look more sophisticated. They might come in the form of bitterness, anger, avoidance, meltdowns at the end of the day, or something similar. They might also be caused by more serious issues like the desire for a husband, child, job, or relationship. But the root cause of them is often the same: we don't get what we want.

We expect life to turn out a certain way. Then, when it doesn't, we get angry at God, ourselves, life in general, or someone close to us.

I'm one of those people who had my life planned out as a child. I would marry while in college, then start having kids a few years later. I never once thought about the possibility of not being able to have the kids I envisioned. That was my dream, and I assumed God placed it in my heart and would therefore make it come to pass.

What happens when our dreams don't come to fruition? What happens when what we long for doesn't take place? One biblical figure who provides an amazing example is Hannah.

In 1 Samuel we are told that Hannah longed for a child and waited in agony as God seemed to ignore her requests. What's worse, the Bible even says God closed her womb (1 Samuel 1:6), which means He was directly involved in her suffering. It's one thing for God to allow difficulty into our lives, but it's quite another story for Him to cause it. Why would the God of love actually cause someone such agony?

Though there's no way to know for certain this side of heaven, I have a theory. Maybe God closed Hannah's womb because she wasn't yet ready for the future that awaited her. Maybe He closed her womb to prepare her for the amazing thing that was getting ready to happen to her son.

After all, Samuel grew up to be one of the most amazing prophets who ever lived. He became a prophet because Hannah brought him to live in the temple. She did this, of course, because she knew Samuel was a direct answer to prayer: "I prayed for this child, and the LORD has granted me what I asked of him. So now I give him to the LORD." (1 Samuel 1:27-28)

Maybe God closed Hannah's womb because He saw the bigger picture. He knew Samuel would be an amazing prophet, and He knew the only way to get Hannah to give him back to God was to help her realize her son was an answer to prayer. If she'd had no problem getting pregnant, she may not have been as willing to give her little boy back to God.

Whatever the reason, I do know one thing: When Hannah threw her fit, she threw it at the feet of her Father in heaven. She didn't grow bitter. She didn't turn her back on Him. She didn't give up her faith. Instead, she gave her life and her sorrows to God. And God took notice. We would be wise to follow Hannah's example.

QUESTIONS FOR REFLECTION

1. Do you struggle with this passage of Scripture? Why or why not?
2. What other possible explanations can you think of for why

God closed Hannah's womb?

3. This is a tough question, one that Bible scholars have argued about for centuries. I don't expect you to come to a certain answer, but I would like you to think about it. Do you think God causes pain, or allows it? Explain your answer.

PRAYER

Admit to God any struggles you might have with passages like this one. Admit it's hard to think God closed Hannah's womb, just as it's hard to think about Him causing anyone pain. Ask Him to help you trust Him, even when you don't understand.

SCRIPTURES FOR FURTHER MEDITATION

James 4:1–3, Psalm 107:1–6, 1 Thessalonians 5:17, Luke 18:1–7

JOURNAL ACTIVITY

What did you imagine your life to be like? In your journal, describe the life you pictured. Now, write down a description of the life you have. What things are similar to your ideal? What things are drastically different? What do you think would have happened if you had received the perfect life you imagined? Do you think you would still depend on God as much as you do now? Do you think you would be the same person you are today? Write in your journal your thoughts to these questions. Then list some of the benefits to *not* getting everything you want.

TAKEAWAY

When God seems late, throw your fit at the feet of Jesus.

Abram and Sarai

Scripture reading: Genesis 15:1–6 and 16:1–3

> *"Look up at the sky and count the stars —*
> *if indeed you can count them... So shall*
> *your offspring be." — Genesis 15:5*

Some things get better with time. The most delicious steak I have ever eaten was what they called aged. Clothes and shoes are more comfortable after they are worn over and over again. Few things compare to the feel of a good pair of jeans that are slightly frayed at the knees or back pockets.

Some things are better with age, but childbirth is *not* one of them. Neither is a promise unfulfilled. Abram and Sarai had both.

Having a baby at an advanced age is not my idea of fun. I don't know anyone who would choose to have a baby at 100 years of age. My guess is, that wasn't Abram's ideal situation either. I also don't know anyone who would enjoy waiting several decades for someone to keep his or her promise.

Waiting, though, is exactly what God asked Abram and Sarai to do. Apparently, God wanted them to be good and "aged" before they brought their child into the world.

In Genesis 12, when God first promised Abram he would become a great nation, Abram was seventy-five years old. Isaac wasn't born until twenty-five years later. It's no wonder Abram and Sarai tried to rush the plan. After a few years of no results, they probably began to wonder if God was ever going to keep His promise. They might have even questioned whether they heard His promise correctly. Maybe they only imagined it. Maybe it didn't really happen. Or maybe it did happen, but God wanted them to help the process along.

Those doubts may have been what led Abram and Sarai to take matters into their own hands when Abram was eighty-six. Sarai offered her servant, Hagar, to Abram and planned to claim their child as her own. She probably thought this was how God meant to make her a mother. But it wasn't.

God wanted Abram and Sarai to wait for His timing, not rush God's plan, but because they refused to do so, they faced years of turmoil. An angel of the Lord said Abram and Hagar's son, Ishmael, would "live in hostility toward all his brothers." (Genesis 16:12)

Think of all of the chaos in the Middle East that could have been avoided if Abram and Sarai would have waited on God. Whatever pain they went through could have been prevented if they had trusted God's timing instead of taking their lives into their own hands.

Unfortunately, it's easy to say we follow Jesus, but it's much harder to live it. In Luke 9:23, Jesus said, "Whoever wants to be my disciple must deny themselves and take up their cross daily and follow me."

Taking up a cross isn't about bearing a difficulty. It's about dying to ourselves, daily. To give Him our lives means we have to die to ourselves and sacrifice our plans if they're not in line with God's.

Shortly after Carrie Underwood won *American Idol*, she sang a song called "Jesus Take the Wheel." Abram and Sarai didn't let God drive, at least not in this situation. They might have given Him the wheel for a moment, but they didn't let Him keep steering.

You and I can choose today if we want to give over the wheel. We can give Him control and trust His timing with whatever we are facing, or we can take the wheel from His hands, drive how we want, and hope for the best.

Giving Jesus complete control of our lives is scary, but it's also liberating. Who better than the One who knows the future to trust with your future? Corrie ten Boom said, "Never be afraid to trust an unknown future to a known God." What is around the corner might be scary because we don't know what it holds. Jesus, on the other hand, does know. Trust Him today, friends. He won't lead you wrong.

QUESTIONS FOR REFLECTION

1. You would have to be pretty desperate to give your husband to another woman. How do you imagine Sarai felt before she

made the decision to let Hagar go to Abram?

2. Why is it so hard to give God complete control of your life?

PRAYER

Ask God to help you wait on Him. Then read Psalm 27:14, which says, "Wait for the LORD; be strong and take heart and wait for the LORD." Ask God to give you patience and help you leave the steering wheel of your life in His hands, where it belongs.

SCRIPTURES FOR FURTHER MEDITATION

Psalm 27:14, Lamentations 3:24–26, Micah 7:7, Psalm 130:5–6

JOURNAL ACTIVITY

Trace your handprint in your journal. Then write beside it, "My life is in *His* hands."

TAKEAWAY

When God seems late, refuse to take matters into your own hands.

Jairus

Scripture reading: Luke 8:40–56

"Then a man named Jairus, a synagogue leader, came and fell at Jesus' feet, pleading with him to come to his house because his only daughter, a girl of about twelve, was dying." — Luke 8:41–42

On Good Friday last spring, my sons were playing outside. My five-year-old son was playing golf in the backyard while my two-year-old explored the yard looking for bugs. One moment he was a safe distance from the golf practice. Then I looked away and a few moments later heard the most awful sound: metal blasting into a head. Wham!

My two-year-old had walked behind his brother and got creamed right above his left eye with a golf club, leaving a massive gash on his forehead. This golf club wasn't one of those five-dollar plastic kid's toys you purchase at the toy store. No, this club was the real stuff. Solid, heavy metal. Metal that could do a lot of damage to a little boy's face.

My two-year-old wailed as blood streamed down his face. I'll never forget the way he looked as he ran to me for comfort. His eyes were locked on mine, and he couldn't get to me fast enough. I couldn't take away his pain or turn back time to prevent the accident, but that wasn't what he focused on in that moment. What he focused on was getting to the one who could kiss his boo-boos and make everything better.

I think most children, unless they have been through abuse or neglect or some other traumatic experience, do the same thing instinctively. When they get hurt, they run to their mom or dad. It's almost as if they know we can make things better. We are the ones who kiss their boo-boos when they are toddlers, who take them to the doctor when they are sick, and who pray over their injuries when we can't do anything else to help. They run to us because they know we have at least a little bit of power to help.

Jairus, when his daughter was sick, ran to the One who had *all* the power. Jesus didn't call a doctor when someone came to Him for help. He was the doctor. He reached into His immeasurable power supply and healed. Or, at least, that's what He often did. At other times, it seemed He didn't make it on time. This was the case with Jairus.

Jairus came to Jesus and fell at His feet, begging Him to heal his twelve-year-old daughter who was near death. Jesus agreed to go with Jairus to his home. On their way, though, something distracted them. A woman who had bled for twelve years reached out to touch Jesus, hoping that touching Him might heal her. Jesus knew power left Him when she touched Him so He stopped the crowd. "Who touched me?" he asked. (Luke 8:45)

Can you imagine what was going through Jairus' mind? *Who cares who touched you? Why are we stopping? We need to get home — fast! Time is running out.* If he had a watch, I imagine he would have anxiously looked down, fearing they wouldn't make it home in time.

His fears were well-founded. A few minutes later some men came to Jairus and told him his worst fear had come to pass. His daughter was dead.

Jairus had a choice to make. He could have gotten angry with Jesus: *If You would have hurried, we might have made it on time!* He could have gotten angry with the woman: *It's your fault we didn't make it!* Or he could have continued to believe Jesus was able. He could have believed that even when God seems late, He can still do miracles.

Because Jairus chose to follow this path and to continue to believe, his little girl was brought back to life.

Today, whatever you are facing, you also have a choice. You can choose to become bitter and angry because God isn't moving as fast as you would like, or you can keep running to Him. Jairus ran to Jesus when he needed a miracle; will you run to Him too?

QUESTIONS FOR REFLECTION

1. If you were Jairus, how would you have felt when Jesus stopped to help the woman?

2. Jairus was a synagogue leader. That means it was probably somewhat risky for him to associate with Jesus. The other religious leaders didn't like Jesus and wanted nothing more than for Him to be silenced. They certainly didn't want to give His followers any more reason to believe in Him. How does knowing this background about Jairus make his actions even more impressive?

PRAYER

Run to Jesus in your prayer today. Bring everything you have been carrying to His feet. Just as Jairus trusted Jesus even when it seemed all hope was gone, pray you will trust Him as well.

SCRIPTURES FOR FURTHER MEDITATION

1 Peter 5:7, Psalm 55:22, Matthew 6:25–34

JOURNAL ACTIVITY

Write the following verse in your journal: "Cast all your anxiety on him because he cares for you." (1 Peter 5:7) Then work on adding this verse to your memory.

TAKEAWAY

When God seems late, run to Him anyway.

When God Doesn't Save

We all want God to save us from our trials, but what happens if He doesn't? What happens if He chooses to let our storms rage? There's a quote that's been floating around online that says, "Sometimes God calms the storm, and sometimes He calms his child."[1]

When I face a trial, I would much rather God calm the storm around me and remove the trial. It's easier that way, and I prefer easy over hard. Sadly, God doesn't always do that. Sometimes, for whatever reason, He chooses not to remove the storm.

This week, we're going to talk about what we can do when He chooses *not* to calm the storm, but instead to calm His children. We'll look at Daniel and Shadrach, Meshach, and Abednego, whom God allowed to walk through terrifying situations. We'll also study the lives of Jesus and Paul, two men who understood what it was like for God to choose *not* to save them from something painful. Lastly, we'll look at Jesus' parable about the rich man and Lazarus.

In each of these biblical accounts, God was capable of preventing pain but chose not to do so. Let's find out why.

After you complete this week's lessons, please watch the video at...

www.crossrivermedia.com/portfolio/unbeaten-week-four

Daniel

Scripture reading: Daniel 6:1–28

*"So the king gave the order, and they brought
Daniel and threw him into the lions' den.
The king said to Daniel, 'May your God, whom
you serve continually, rescue you!'" — Daniel 6:16*

Several years ago, I went through Beth Moore's Daniel Bible study. As I was preparing to write today's devotional, I looked back through that book. On the margins of each week's session I wrote prayer requests. One name showed up on these lists over and over again through the twelve-week study — Sonny.

Sonny is my husband's uncle. When he was forty-seven years old, shortly after my Bible study ended, he passed away, leaving behind a wife of twenty-seven years and two children in their early twenties.

As I read his name in my lists of prayer requests, one thought kept running through my mind — God didn't save Sonny. Even though I, along with many others, prayed for him for weeks on end, God didn't save him. The all-powerful God, who created the universe and crafted animals, lakes, and trees out of nothing, didn't save Sonny from death, even though He was capable of doing so.

Maybe you or a loved one prayed for God's healing touch, and He didn't heal. Or maybe you prayed for Him to spare you from something, and He said no.

For the next few days, we're going to look at several biblical figures God didn't save… or at least, didn't save in the way we expected. For this first week, let's look at the life of Daniel.

Daniel was one of the Israelites taken from Jerusalem when King Nebuchadnezzar of Babylon attacked the city. Even after he was taken captive, Daniel remained faithful to God. When other Israelites chose to follow the orders of the king and eat whatever they were given, Daniel and some of his friends risked the anger of the king by rejecting this food because they didn't want to defile themselves.

Daniel and his buddies again showed their faithfulness when Nebuchadnezzar threatened to kill the wise men because they could not interpret the king's dream. Instead of giving in to fear, Daniel and his friends got on their knees in prayer.

We find even more evidence of Daniel's faithfulness when his enemies tried to trap him and couldn't. They finally concluded, "We will never find any basis for charges against this man Daniel unless it has something to do with the law of his God." (Daniel 6:5)

His enemies plotted against him and asked the king to decree that no one could pray to anyone or anything except the king for the next thirty days. The king made the edict and sealed Daniel's fate because our faithful follower of God would not stop praying, even when he knew his prayers could lead to a death sentence. He got down on his knees, like he had always done, and prayed to God three times a day.

When Daniel's enemies saw him, they challenged the king to follow through with his command and give Daniel the punishment his "crime" deserved: imprisonment in the lions' den.

Now at this point in Daniel's story, I'm crying for justice. Daniel did nothing wrong! Save him, God! I'm thinking of ways I would have saved him. I may have made the men carrying Daniel fall into the pit themselves, as Daniel miraculously leaped over the hole of the den. Or make the lions magically disappear. When the lid of the den was opened, presto! No lions! Or I might have helped the king of Babylon come up with some way he didn't have to follow the edict.

What I wouldn't have done is let Daniel, my faithful and obedient child, be thrown into the den. I wouldn't have allowed him to go through the torture of contemplating his own death as he fell from the hands of his enemies towards the mouths of hungry lions. Somehow, I would have saved him.

But then, it's a good thing I'm not God, because Daniel would have missed an even more amazing miracle. Because God let Daniel fall into the lions' den, Daniel got to witness an angel hold the lions' hungry, salivating mouths closed. Because God let Daniel go into the den of lions, King Darius issued a new decree that everyone should praise the God of Daniel. And because God allowed Daniel to walk with lions, God's name was glorified and Daniel was held in high honor.

I still don't know why God didn't save Sonny from death. From my perspective, it doesn't make sense, but I am looking at it from an earthly perspective. Being saved from something doesn't mean it doesn't happen to you. From God's perspective, it might mean that even if something does happen to you, you're not alone in the fight. There are really three ways to be saved: for God to prevent something from happening, for God to let that something happen but then heal you of it, or for God to heal you after that something looks like it won.[2]

That third way is how God saved Sonny. God didn't prevent his death, as we all would have liked, but God did save him by allowing his death to purge his earthly body of disease. There's one thing I know for sure about my husband's uncle: there is not even the tiniest bit of disease in his body now.

QUESTIONS FOR REFLECTION

1. Why do you think God didn't stop Daniel from being thrown into the den of lions?
2. What are you praying for God to save you from right now?

PRAYER

Pray for God to give you courage as you face your trials. Ask Him to give you faith like Daniel's that even a lions' den can't destroy.

SCRIPTURES FOR FURTHER MEDITATION

2 Timothy 1:7–8, Ephesians 6:10–20

JOURNAL ACTIVITY

In your journal, write the three ways God saves:

1. By preventing something from happening.
2. By allowing something to happen but healing you from it.
3. By healing you after that something looks like it's won.

TAKEAWAY

When God doesn't save in this life,
don't forget He's still saving in the next.

Shadrach, Meshach and Abednego

Scripture reading: Daniel 3:1–30

"If we are thrown into the blazing furnace, the God we serve is able to deliver us from it, and he will deliver us from Your Majesty's hand. But even if he does not, we want you to know, Your Majesty, that we will not serve your gods or worship the image of gold you have set up." — Daniel 3:17–18

What if God doesn't fix your problem?

Of course, I hope He does. I hope He heals your body, provides a spouse, grants you the child you long for, provides a job, or whatever it is you want Him to do. But what if He doesn't?

What if, for whatever reason, God chooses not to heal your body? It's one thing to trust God when He answers your prayers; it's a whole different story to trust Him when He says no or doesn't say a thing at all. Will you remain faithful even if your greatest fears come to pass?

This is the question Shadrach, Meshach, and Abednego each had to answer. If God didn't save them, would they still follow Him? Yesterday, we studied the life of Daniel, one of the faithful Israelites who was taken captive by King Nebuchadnezzar. When Daniel was taken captive, other Israelites were taken with him. Three of these men were Shadrach, Meshach, and Abednego. Like Daniel, these three men chose to cling to God through difficult circumstances. In Daniel 3, King Nebuchadnezzar ordered the citizens of his kingdom to bow down to a golden image he had created. Anyone who refused would be thrown into a fiery furnace.

Most of the people living in Nebuchadnezzar's kingdom obeyed. They didn't want to face the rage of a man who was known for being hasty with his sword. Three men, however, refused to bow their faces to the ground in front of an idol. Shadrach, Meshach, and Abednego believed God could save them from the hands of Nebuchadnezzar and from the fire.

These men standing up to the king who held their lives in his hands is amazing in itself. Even more amazing is that these men realized God might not save them — and were okay with that! Even if God does not save us, they said to the king, we will not serve your gods (Daniel 3:18).

Impressive faith, huh? Because of this bold proclamation, I expected God to save the men. If I had been He, I certainly would have. With a speech like that, these men deserved to avoid the heat. Apparently, though, God didn't see it that way. Instead of saving them *from* the fire, He chose to save them *through* the fire.[3]

Yesterday, I shared three ways God saves His followers: by preventing something from happening, by allowing it but rescuing us from it, and by ultimately saving us in eternity. In this story, God chose option two. He didn't prevent the fire, but saved through it instead. Isaiah 43:2 says...

"When you pass through the waters, I will be with you; and when you pass through the rivers, they will not sweep over you. When you walk through the fire, you will not be burned; the flames will not set you ablaze."

Nebuchadnezzar ordered the fire heated seven times hotter than usual. Then he had the three men bound and thrown in. The furnace was so hot it killed the soldiers. Shadrach, Meshach, and Abednego, in contrast, weren't harmed at all. The flames did not singe their hair, and the text says they didn't even smell like smoke.

When Nebuchadnezzar saw the men walking around in the fire that killed his soldiers, he jumped to his feet and said, "Look! I see four men walking around in the fire, unbound and unharmed, and the fourth looks like a son of the gods." (Daniel 3:25)

God didn't prevent Shadrach, Meshach, and Abednego from being thrown into the fire. What He did instead was join them there.

That might be what He does for us too. He might not prevent the fire, but He will join us in it. He'll walk with us on the hot coals and make sure not one hair on our heads gets singed. He'll make sure when we leave the fire, there's not even a smoke smell lingering on our clothes.

QUESTIONS FOR REFLECTION

1. Why do you think God didn't save Shadrach, Meshach, and Abednego *from* the fire?
2. What are the benefits of having gone through a fire?
3. What fire are you facing right now?

PRAYER

Pray for the God of Shadrach, Meshach, and Abednego to give you faith like these men. Pray you will be able to say, as these men did, "Even if you don't take this away from me, I will still follow you." Ask God to fill in any faith gaps that exist in your life.

SCRIPTURES FOR FURTHER MEDITATION

Psalm 46:1–3, Psalm 119:50, Isaiah 43:2

JOURNAL ACTIVITY

Read Daniel 3. Then answer this question: Are you willing to follow God, even if He doesn't take away the painful situation you are currently facing? If you're willing, write on the cover of your journal the words, "*even if.*" Every time you look at those words, remind yourself of your commitment to follow God, even if He doesn't save you from the trials in your life.

TAKEAWAY

When God doesn't save, look for Him in your fire
and search for His footprints in the ashes.

The Rich Man and Lazarus

Scripture reading: Luke 16:19–31

"The time came when the beggar died and the angels carried him to Abraham's side. The rich man also died and was buried." — Luke 16:22

Diann was a young mother of five children when she was diagnosed with cancer. Her youngest son was born just five months before her diagnosis. If anyone had reason to be saved from death, it was Diann. Her five small children needed her, and her husband who traveled for several months out of the year needed her. It didn't make sense for God *not* to save this woman from cancer.

After her diagnosis, Diann went to the hospital for exploratory surgery. After surgery, the doctor told her husband, "Robin, I don't see any hope for Diann."⁴ The cancer had filled her entire body and was quickly ravaging the few healthy cells that remained. Robin and Diann called for prayer to anyone and everyone who was willing. Because Robin traveled often, the call went far. They begged God to heal her of the cancer that threatened both her life and her husband's faith.

Despite their prayers, God chose not to heal her. She fought bravely for several years, but in the end, went home to be with her Savior. Her youngest son was only three years old.

Robin admitted later he yelled at God when he first heard his wife's diagnosis, threatening to never serve Him again.

Have you been there? Have you told God that if this is what someone who serves Him gets, then you want no part of it? Ever threatened to turn your back on Him because of the things He allowed into your life?

Diann didn't deserve death. Her husband didn't deserve to be left a widower with five young children to raise alone, and her children didn't deserve to grow up without a mother. From our limited perspective, God should have saved her.

So what do you do when God who is powerful enough to prevent the catastrophe in your life chooses not to stop it? When He chooses to allow the tornado, car accident, or bankruptcy — what then?

Jesus told a parable in Luke 16 that gives us insight into one thing we can do when these things happen. The story was about two men: a poor man named Lazarus (not to be confused with the brother to Mary and Martha) and a rich, unnamed man.

Jesus said that on this earth, the rich man had everything he could ever need. He dressed in purple like royalty and lived in luxury (Luke 16:19). He had everything money could buy. Lazarus, on the other hand, had nothing. He sat at the gate of the rich man and begged for the rich man's scraps. Covered with sores from head to toe, Lazarus' belly might have been swollen from hunger. He was the picture of depravity.

Eventually, both of the men died. Lazarus went to heaven, and the rich man went to hell. While the rich man was in torture, he looked up and saw Lazarus with Abraham and begged him to provide just a drop of cold water to cool his burning tongue. Abraham replied, "Son, remember that in your lifetime you received your good things, while Lazarus received bad things, but now he is comforted here and you are in agony." (Luke 16:25)

While we are on this earth, it is easy to get caught up in the here-and-now. It's easy to only see what's right in front of us — our pain, the things we wish we had, and the blessings others have that make us wonder why God doesn't bless equally. We get caught up in this life and forget there's so much more to come in the life to follow.

Though this side of eternity feels like a long time while we are in it, it is really only a dot on the timeline of our existence. I want to challenge you today to focus your attention on the life to come. Don't allow the difficulties in this short life to keep you from obtaining the blessings of the life that will last forever.

When Diann knew she was about to die, she called each of her children to her lap and gave them one final challenge. "Be there," she told them. Diann thought of heaven, even in her dying moments. Even through the most difficult of circumstances, she kept her eyes heavenward — and asked her kids to do the same. Can I challenge you to do likewise?

QUESTIONS FOR REFLECTION

1. Why is it so difficult to think about eternity?
2. What steps can you take to help you think about eternity more often?

PRAYER

Pray for God to give you eyes that see more than what's going on in your life today. Ask Him to give you His heavenward perspective.

SCRIPTURES FOR FURTHER MEDITATION

Philippians 3:20–21, 2 Corinthians 5:1–9

JOURNAL ACTIVITY

Write Colossians 3:2 in your journal. Then work on memorizing it throughout the week. "Set your minds on things above, not on earthly things."

TAKEAWAY

When God doesn't save, instead of focusing on
the life you are struggling through right now,
fix your eyes on the life that will last forever.

Jesus

*"God made him who had no sin to be
sin for us, so that in him we might become the
righteousness of God." — 2 Corinthians 5:21*

Every Christmas, Easter, and Valentine's Day, as I grew up, my mom made sure my brothers and I all received the same kind of candy in our stockings or baskets. What's more (and what we still tease my mom about) is that she made sure we even got the same amount of each color of candy.

For instance, we each got twelve red Skittles, ten yellow ones, seven green ones, and eleven orange ones. If one of us got thirteen red Skittles and another eleven, we cried *"unfair!"* and wanted my mom to make it right. God bless her for loving us so much, and bearing with us as we sought to make everything in life fair.

It starts early, doesn't it, this desire for life to be fair? Even my two-year-old wants everything in his world to be fair. If his older brother gets to stay up ten minutes late at bedtime, he thinks he should get to stay up late also. If his older brother doesn't have to hold my hand when walking on the sidewalk, he shouldn't have to either.

Even as adults, we want life to be fair. It makes sense, then, that when something goes wrong in our lives, one of the first things we cry for is justice. We don't think we deserve this, and we want God to make it right. Sometimes, we even demand He make it right.

I have certainly struggled with this type of thinking. I deserve a baby. I would be a great mother. I would be a better mother than those women who deliver their babies in restrooms and then leave them there to die. You give them babies, God, and they don't even take care of them. Why not me? It's just not fair.

Maybe everyone around you seems to get everything they want. It seems like you are the only one whom God is holding out on. He gives freely to others with open arms. Another baby? Of course. I'll even make this one the girl you've been longing for... A raise at work? It's coming next week... A healthy family? Absolutely... But for you, His hands seemed clenched shut. Everything you pray for, He refuses. The very things He gives freely to others are the things He won't allow you to grasp.

We cry for God's justice because we assume if God were fair, He would give us the things we desire. We assume we deserve to have our prayers answered with a resounding yes. The problem is, our thinking is flawed. If God were fair, we wouldn't get everything we want. We'd all get hell. Each and every one of us. That is what we deserve. Romans 3:23 says, "all have sinned and fall short of the glory of God."

All of us deserve hell. Is it hard when God seems to give generously to others and withhold from us? Of course it's hard. But fairness isn't the answer. If God were fair, Jesus wouldn't have died on a wooden cross 2000 years ago, because Jesus did nothing wrong. He did nothing deserving of death. If God were fair, Jesus wouldn't have been the one up on that death trap. You and I would have been.

If we're really honest, you and I don't want fair. Not really. What we want is easy. We want a life that's free of pain, tears, and difficulties. We want a life that gives us what we want and fulfills all our dreams and hopes. Friends, that was never the life Jesus promised. Jesus promised in this world we would have trouble (John 16:33). He didn't promise a life of ease.

In Matthew 7, Jesus told the story of two men who built homes. One built his home on the rock. The other built his on the sand. When the rains came, only the house built on the rock stood firm. The other collapsed under the force of the storm. What I want to point out about this story is that both homes faced storms. God didn't keep the rain away from either one, just as He might not keep the hard things from us who follow Him. The storms are going to come, both to the faithful and to the unfaithful. No one is exempt.

God didn't promise easy. He promised hope, joy, and peace — yes — but not the absence of pain.

75

QUESTIONS FOR REFLECTION

1. Why do you think we often want life to be fair?
2. Do you agree or disagree with this: "If we're really being honest, you and I don't want fair. Not really. What we want is easy." Explain your answer.

PRAYER

Thank God for being unfair in His treatment of Jesus. Jesus didn't deserve death and yet that's what God gave Him because of His great love for us. Spend time giving God thanks for that amazing love.

SCRIPTURES FOR MEDITATION

Romans 3:23–26, 1 Peter 2:24, Isaiah 53, 2 Corinthians 5:21

JOURNAL ACTIVITY

Draw a picture of a cross in your journal. Below it, write this prayer: "Thank you, God, for not being fair."

TAKEAWAY

When God doesn't save, don't cry for Him to be fair.
Thank Him for being unfair with Jesus.

Paul

Scripture reading: 2 Corinthians 12:7–9

*"I was given a thorn in my flesh, a messenger
of Satan, to torment me. Three times I pleaded
with the Lord to take it away from me. But he said
to me, 'My grace is sufficient for you, for my power is
made perfect in weakness.'"* — 2 Corinthians 12:7–9

A few months ago, my five-year-old son got a monster of a splinter. This thing wasn't a tiny piece of wood that was stuck beneath his skin. No, it was like a small twig, and was buried so deep I could barely get to it with tweezers. As my son wailed in pain, I desperately tried to remove the wood as quickly as possible.

Whatever I had been doing was now at the bottom of my to-do list. The only thing that mattered to me was getting that splinter out of my son's little hand so he wouldn't hurt any longer.

It makes me wonder why God did *not* take the thorn out of Paul's flesh in 2 Corinthians 12? How could God *not* grab His metaphorical tweezers and tug on that thing until it came out of Paul's tortured skin?

There are a variety of theories of what his thorn in the flesh was. Some suggest it was a disease like malaria or epilepsy. Others say it was some sort of problem with his eyes. Some believe it was a temptation. Though we don't know what the thorn was, we do know it caused Paul a lot of agony. He begged God to remove it, but God didn't take it away.

One thing that is interesting about this is that Paul might have been more effective if he didn't have this thorn in the flesh. If it was a disease, it probably prevented him from preaching or traveling occasionally. It might have made him weak physically, thus making it harder for him to share the gospel. It's possible Paul's ministry would have been more effective if he didn't have the thorn.

Why, then, did God choose to leave it? When Paul begged for it to be removed and when its very presence hindered the gospel, why did God leave this thing in Paul's skin to fester? It makes much more sense to us to remove the painful thorn and let Paul get back to doing what he did best: preaching the truth of Jesus Christ.

On the other hand, perhaps Paul's ministry wouldn't have been better without the thorn. Maybe the thorn made his ministry more effective or made Paul more compassionate. It could be that the thorn made Paul learn to be content in all situations, which made his message that much more powerful.

In Isaiah 38:17, Isaiah said these words, "Surely it was for my benefit that I suffered such anguish." I wonder if Paul would agree. Maybe his thorn, though painful and frustrating, was actually a blessing in disguise, a blessing because God used it to refine Paul's character.

I don't know what your thorn is, but chances are it makes your testimony more effective. He may have allowed it to stick around because He knew you would choose to use it for the Kingdom. The question is... are you willing to put up with the thorn so God can use it? If you had to choose between a less effective but thorn-free life or a more effective, thorny life, what would you choose? These are hard questions, but we would be wise to consider them.

In verse seven, Paul told the Corinthians why God left the thorn in his flesh. He said it kept him from becoming conceited about all of the revelations God gave him. It's easy to understand why Paul might have been conceited. His history as a Pharisee was impeccable. He had literally been called out by God to be the minister to the Gentiles. He wrote a huge chunk of the New Testament. Paul could have easily looked at his résumé and concluded, "Look at all I've done." So it seems God left the thorn because He was more concerned with Paul's character than making Paul's life comfortable.

If I'm being completely honest, this is hard for me. At times, I would prefer an easy life to one that builds my character. At times, I long for the thorn-free version of my story. Here's the thing, though. The thorn-free version of my story might be more comfortable, but it won't be nearly as powerful. God's no might leave a splinter in my skin, but if I'll let Him, He'll use that splinter to craft me into the woman He designed me to be. His no might be more painful than His yes, but He knows what He's doing. The question is, will I accept His no, just as quickly as I'd accept His yes?

QUESTIONS FOR REFLECTION

1. How might God be using your thorn to make your testimony more powerful?
2. Are you willing to accept God's no? Spend time today thinking and praying about this question.

PRAYER

Ask God to mold your character through your thorn. Ask Him to use it for His glory and for your betterment. Pray for God to help you accept His no just as you would accept His yes.

SCRIPTURES FOR FURTHER MEDITATION

Isaiah 38:17, 2 Kings 20:1–11, 2 Corinthians 1:3–5,
Romans 5:3–5, Hebrews 12:11

JOURNAL ACTIVITY

Brainstorm some ways Paul's thorn might have made him into a better person. List all of your thoughts in your journal. Then consider how God might use your thorn to mold you into the person He longs for you to become.

TAKEAWAY

When God doesn't save, let Him use the thorn to mold your character.

When Bad Things Happen to Good People

n Psalm 73, Asaph shares what I think many of us have thought before about the wicked:

"They have no struggles; their bodies are healthy and strong. They are free from common human burdens; they are not plagued by human ills.... This is what the wicked are like — always free of care, they go on amassing wealth. Surely in vain I have kept my heart pure and have washed my hands in innocence. All day long I have been afflicted, and every morning brings new punishments." (Psalm 73:4-14)

Bad things happen to good people, and good things happen to bad. My children say it's just not fair. Can you relate? Do you wonder why God seems to bless the wicked and withhold from the godly?

For the next five days, we'll explore the lives of five good people who didn't receive the good things they deserved. We'll study Joseph, Jesus, Hosea, John the Baptist, and Moses, and answer the question, what do you do when bad things happen to good people?

After you complete this week's lessons, please watch the video at...
www.crossrivermedia.com/portfolio/unbeaten-week-five

Joseph

Scripture reading: Genesis 39:1–23

*"But while Joseph was there in the prison,
the L*ORD *was with him…" — Genesis 39:20–21*

I f God were really with me, He wouldn't allow this to happen. We may not say the words aloud, but most of us have thought them at least a time or two. We assume once we decide to follow Jesus Christ, he will keep certain things from our lives. He might allow us to get sick, but He won't allow us to get cancer. He might not stop us from getting in a car wreck, but He will stop our child from being killed in that accident. In other words, there are certain trials that are off limits for believers.

After all, God is a loving Father, and no loving parent would ever allow his or her child to get cancer or lose a loved one. At least, that's what we assume, because we wouldn't allow our children to go through such difficult circumstances. If we had the power to stop our child from getting sick, we'd use that power to heal. If we had the power to prevent his or her pain and suffering, we'd prevent it, and it baffles us when God doesn't always use His power to protect us from pain.

The problem with this mindset is it's not at all what the Bible teaches. Yes, God is a loving Father, but that doesn't mean He won't allow terrible things into our lives. Jesus promised life would be difficult when he said, "In this world you will have trouble. But take heart! I have overcome the world." (John 16:33) Peter said something similar. "Dear friends, do not be surprised at the fiery ordeal that has come on you to test you, as though something strange were happening to you." (1 Peter 4:12)

God didn't promise comfort. He promised He'd be with us through the hard. For some reason, though, we believe the lie that discipleship equals comfort. It doesn't.

A survey of biblical heroes proves following God doesn't guarantee a carefree life. In fact, sometimes it guarantees the opposite — pain and difficulties. We've already looked at several of these heroes of the faith. Remember Job and Paul, Esther and Stephen, and Daniel and Jesus. Each of these followed after the Father, and none of them received a life of ease. Another biblical hero who had a painful life was Joseph.

He was a man who lived with integrity. So much so, in fact, that when an opportunity to sin fell into his lap in the form of a beautiful woman, he refused. Joseph literally ran from his temptation, leaving his coat behind. As I read this story, I can't help but cheer for this incredible young man. If his story were a play, I think he'd receive a standing ovation as he darted off stage. "Way to go, Joseph!" the crowds might cheer. We expect the same treatment from God. Surely God would reward him for his faithfulness.

Instead of a reward, however, he received a prison cell. The woman Joseph rejected accused our hero of molesting her, and as a result he went to jail, not because he sinned, but because he refused to sin. His faithfulness, rather than protecting him from pain, actually caused it.

If anyone had reason to believe God had left him, it was Joseph. No one would blame him for questioning God's presence after what he went through. His brothers abused him and sold him into slavery, and his master threw him in prison for a crime he didn't commit. From outward appearances, it sure looked as though God was no longer with him.

But the text says something completely different. "While Joseph was there in the prison, the LORD was with him." (Genesis 39:20-21) It says similar words a few verses earlier about Joseph's time as a servant. "The LORD was with Joseph so that he prospered, and he lived in the house of his Egyptian master." (Genesis 39:2)

God didn't change Joseph's circumstances. He was with Joseph in the prison and in the house of his Egyptian master. The text would have made more sense if it said something like, "God was with Joseph, so He freed him from slavery," or "God was with Joseph, so He released him from jail." But the Bible doesn't say those things. Instead, it says God was with Joseph, right where he was.

Circumstances aren't the best indicators of whether or not God is with us. In fact, at times they might lead us to believe God has left us stranded and is no longer working in our lives. When this happens, we have to remember Joseph, the man who had every reason to believe God was no longer with him, but chose to believe the truth instead. The truth that God is still with us, even when it doesn't feel like it.

There's a verse in Hebrews I read a couple of weeks ago that blew me away. "During the days of Jesus' life on earth, he offered up prayers and petitions with fervent cries and tears to the one who could save him from death, and he was heard because of his reverent submission." (Hebrews 5:7). It is a verse I had read many times before, but this time it struck me. Jesus prayed for God to save Him from the cross, but, as we know, God didn't rescue Him. Instead, He left His child to die. What this verse tells us is that even though God didn't stop the death, He heard the prayer. Jesus "was heard" it says.

God has heard you too. Today and every other day you've called on His name. He may not change your circumstances, you may still have a battle ahead of you, but I promise, He has heard you. Psalm 9:10 promises, "You, LORD, have never forsaken those who seek you." He never has and He never will.

QUESTIONS FOR REFLECTION

1. What are some of the off limit trials in your mind?
2. Why do you think Christian people sometimes believe the lie that God won't allow certain problems into our lives?

PRAYER

Ask God to strengthen your faith when it grows weak. Ask Him to help you see His presence in your life, even when your circumstances suggest otherwise.

SCRIPTURES FOR FURTHER MEDITATION

1 Peter 4:12, Psalm 9:9–10, Psalm 34:19, Psalm 139:7–10

JOURNAL ACTIVITY

Write John 16:33 in your journal: "I have told you these things, so that in me you may have peace. In this world you will have trouble. But take heart! I have overcome the world."

TAKEAWAY

When bad things happen to good people, remain faithful.

Jesus

Scripture reading: Matthew 26:36–46

*"Whoever claims to live in him must
live as Jesus did." — 1 John 2:6*

D o you remember when WWJD bracelets were popular? I was in junior high school and just *had* to have one. Actually, I wanted several in a variety of colors to go with every outfit I wore.

The bracelets asked the question, What Would Jesus Do? They were physical reminders to live like Him throughout the day.

The bracelets are out of vogue, but the goal of the believer is the same: to live like Jesus, or as Ephesians 5:1 says, to "follow God's example."

The question is, how can we follow Jesus' example when bad things happen to good people? Jesus, more than anyone else who ever walked this earth, was a good man to whom bad things happened. He was perfect — sinless. He was the only one who could honestly cry to God, "This isn't fair!" and be right. That is why it is so important to look at Jesus' response to His suffering. He did three things when He knew His death on the cross was approaching.

The first thing He did was pray. In Matthew 26, right before Judas handed Jesus over to the religious leaders, Jesus went to the Garden of Gethsemane to talk to His Father. He told His disciples, "My soul is overwhelmed with sorrow to the point of death." Then "he fell with his face to the ground and prayed." (Matthew 26:38–39)

Some of us do this naturally. When we face a difficult situation, we go to the Lord in prayer before we do anything else. Others of us, especially if we feel God has let us down in the past, are hesitant to bring another request before Him. What if He doesn't answer again or worse yet, what if He does answer, and I don't like the answer? Jesus didn't give in to those questions. When He faced an unfair trial, He brought it before His Father in prayer.

Jesus also submitted to the Father's will. After He fell on His face before God, He said these powerful words, "My Father, if it is possible, may this cup be taken from me. *Yet not as I will, but as you will.*" (Matthew 26:39, emphasis mine) Jesus didn't want to go to the cross. He begged God to come up with another way to bring salvation to the world. But when His Father said no, Jesus submitted Himself to God's plan.

A few weeks ago, I attended a conference for moms, ministry leaders, and mentors. During the conference, one of the speakers challenged the audience to surrender their plans to God. She dared us to let go of the plans we were clinging to and grab hold of God's plan for our lives.

As I sat and asked God to help me do it in regard to my desire for children, Satan whispered in my ear, "But what if God's plan is painful? It was painful for Jesus, you know. What if His plan for you is painful too and His plan is that you'll never get the one thing for which you long?"

I didn't have an answer for Satan then, and I don't have one now. I don't know if God's plan includes us getting a baby. I don't know if His plan is painful. But I do know this. If God's plan is painful, He will help me through the pain and use it somehow for my good. If His plan hurts, it's because there's something better on the other side of the pain.

A third thing Jesus did when He faced the most unfair event imaginable is He cried out to God. As He hung on the cross and tried to pull His body up enough to catch His breath, He cried out, "My God, my God, why have you forsaken me?" (Matthew 27:46)

With these words, Jesus cried out to the One who put Him there. The cross was God's plan from the beginning. It was the reason Jesus came to this earth. Regardless, even though God the Father was the One who planned the pain, God the Son still called out to Him. Jesus endured the pain because He knew what was coming next. He knew what His Father had waiting for Him on the other side of His death.

We can have that same confidence. We might not know how His plan is going to unfold for our lives on this side of heaven, but we do know how it's going to unfold on the other side. Eternity awaits us. Nothing Satan throws at us in this life can change that. We have hope, not because of our certainty in this life, but because of our certainty in the next.

Hebrews 12:2 says Jesus endured the cross for the joy set before him. Today, can I challenge you to follow His example — to pray to the Father when times get hard, to submit to God's plan, and to cry out to Him even if it's His plan that is hurting your heart?

WWJD bracelets might have only been a fad, but this call to be like Jesus is not going anywhere. Sometimes, being like Him means submitting to a painful plan. The question is, are you willing to submit?

QUESTIONS FOR REFLECTION

1. Which of Jesus' three responses to pain is the hardest for you to do? Why?
2. Do you willingly submit to God's plan, even if it's different than yours?

PRAYER

Pray for God to give you the courage to face your trials as Jesus did. Ask Him to help you pray, submit, and cry out to Him, even when you believe His plan is breaking your heart.

SCRIPTURES FOR FURTHER MEDITATION

Romans 12:1–2, 1 Corinthians 11:1, Ephesians 5:1

JOURNAL ACTIVITY

In your journal, write 1 John 2:6: "Whoever claims to live in him must live as Jesus did." Then list Jesus' three responses to pain. Circle the response you have the hardest time imitating.

TAKEAWAY

When bad things happen to good people, follow Jesus' example.

Moses

Scripture reading: Exodus 1:1–2:10

*"The L*ORD* would speak to Moses face to face,
as one speaks to a friend." — Exodus 33:11*

One of the most horrific historical events was the Holocaust, when Adolf Hitler and the military forces under his command killed approximately eleven million people. Between 1941 and 1945, Hitler and the Nazis targeted Jews and other minority groups. After capturing the victims, the military piled them into freight trains and led them to extermination camps, where they were systematically murdered in gas chambers. It's estimated that approximately six million of the victims of the Holocaust were Jewish, many of them women and children.

Few of us can even imagine what that must have been like… to be a young child taken from his parents and never able to see them again… to be a mother whose children are ripped from her arms… to be a Jew, murdered simply for his heritage. These men, women, and children experienced the worst Plan B imaginable.

They never dreamed when they were little that they would endure any type of genocide, let alone one of this magnitude. Amazingly, many of them maintained their faith in God, even after enduring such an atrocity.

A poet wrote on the walls of one of the concentration camps… "I believe in the sun, even when it is not shining. I believe in love, even when I do not feel it. And I believe in God, even when he is silent."[1]

Whoever wrote this poem was able to find God in his or her Plan B life. Even though his life did not go as planned and even though he did not deserve the excruciating treatment he received, he was able to find God in the midst of it.

Thousands of years before the Holocaust, the Jewish people endured the slaughter of thousands at the hands of another cruel dictator. And it was during that time that another man was born who learned to trust God with what looked like a Plan B life.

In Exodus, the Bible describes a time when the Israelites were living as slaves in Egypt. The Pharoah realized the Jewish people were growing more numerous by the day and he was worried that they would revolt, join his enemies, and fight against his people. So he enslaved them and ordered all the baby boys killed at birth.

It was during this genocide that Moses was born. The midwives who delivered him disobeyed Pharoah's order and chose instead to save those under their care.

Still, Moses had more than his fair share of difficulties. The first three months of his life were spent in hiding. I imagine there were many times when he cried for milk or comfort, only to have a hand placed gently over his mouth. "Not a sound, sweetie. Not a sound," his sister Miriam might have whispered, afraid of being caught.

Years later, after God called Moses to rescue the Israelites from the Egyptians, the people didn't believe him. They questioned his authority and balked at the man God chose to lead them. It was only after God sent plagues upon the Egyptians that the Israelites finally viewed Moses as their chosen leader.

Fast forward a few years, and Moses led the Israelites toward the Promised Land. It appeared things were finally looking up for the people and for Moses. Unfortunately, he lost his temper with the people and disobeyed God in the process (Numbers 20). After a difficult childhood, then urging the Pharaoh to let the people go, leading the grumpy Israelites through the desert, dealing with complaint after complaint from the people, Moses could only look at the Promised Land from a distance. Because of his disobedience, He never went in. Instead, He died in the desert.

What do you think Moses thought his life would be like as a child? I doubt he pictured running from an Egyptian pharoah. I doubt he pictured leading a defiant and whiny group of people through a hot desert for forty years. I doubt he pictured dying in that same desert, just outside of the beautiful land God promised to give his descendants.

Moses' life is the perfect picture of an imperfect Plan B. Still, even though his life didn't go as he might have planned it, His God went with him through a Plan B life.

Exodus 33:11 says, "The LORD would speak to Moses face to face, as one speaks to a friend." While Moses walked in the desert in his Plan B not-what-he-would-have-chosen-for-himself life, God walked with him and spoke to him face to face.

He'll do the same for us. When our Plan A's don't come to pass, He'll come down to meet us in our Plan B and walk with us through our desert.

QUESTIONS FOR REFLECTION

1. What did you hope your life would look like?
2. How is your life different than you originally imagined it would be?

PRAYER

Ask God to go with you through the desert, just as He went with Moses.

SCRIPTURES FOR FURTHER MEDITATION

Joshua 1:9, Deuteronomy 31:6, Psalm 23:4

JOURNAL ACTIVITY

Your life might not have turned out as you thought it would. You might be living in a Plan B right now. Though it is hard at times, my guess is, there are still many things for which you can be thankful. Make a list in your journal of some of these things.

TAKEAWAY

When bad things happen to good people,
let God go with you through the desert.

Hosea

Scripture reading: Hosea 1:1–11, 3:1–3

"When the LORD began to speak through Hosea, the LORD said to him, 'Go, marry a promiscuous woman and have children with her, for like an adulterous wife this land is guilty of unfaithfulness to the LORD." — Hosea 1:2

There are a few famous preachers who might claim God wants you to be happy more than anything else. They say nothing makes Him more pleased than to see us with smiles on our faces, cash in our wallets, and good feelings running through our veins.

I'm guessing these preachers don't spend a lot of time in the book of Hosea. Even a surface reading of it makes it clear the prophet wasn't always happy. If fact, God was the cause of the man's unhappiness.

Hosea was one of God's prophets during the Old Testament times. He spoke to the Israelites when they were rebellious toward God. Instead of seeking Him, they ran after idols and worshipped other gods.

To paint a picture of their rebellion, God told Hosea to marry a promiscuous woman named Gomer. But even after the wedding ceremony, Gomer continued her promiscuous ways. Over and over again, Hosea chased after her for one reason — because God told him to. Even though she ran back into the arms of men who cared nothing for her, Hosea obeyed God and kept going after her. He even dished out cash to buy her back. In chapter 3, verse 1, God told Hosea, "Go, show your love to your wife again, though she is loved by another man and is an adulteress. Love her as the LORD loves the Israelites."

God used Hosea's marriage to Gomer as an object lesson. Just as God loved the rebellious Israelites, Hosea loved his rebellious wife. Just as God kept chasing after rebellious Israel, Hosea kept chasing after unfaithful Gomer. God loved Israel with a never-ending, powerful, unbreakable love that He asked Hosea to portray through a marriage that seemed doomed from the beginning.

The object lesson is powerful. There's no doubt about that.

But what about the prophet whom God used to make His object lesson? Imagine the pain he felt in marrying a woman buried in sin and unwilling to change. Can you imagine giving your life and your heart to someone, only to have it stomped on over and over again? And it was all because the God he followed, the God who is supposed to be loving and good, told him to do it.

It's tempting to read a story like this and think it wasn't hard on Hosea. We tend to forget Hosea was flesh and blood... a person, with the same feelings and emotional needs as you and I. Sure, he was a prophet, but that didn't make him immune to the pain of adultery. It also didn't make him resistant to having his heart broken by a woman he promised to love and cherish. Being a prophet might have made him a godly man, but it didn't exempt him from feeling the judging eyes of family and friends as he vowed himself to a prostitute.

When Hosea obeyed God, he did so at great cost to himself. He may have lost his reputation. After all, what godly man would knowingly marry a prostitute? He could have lost his family and friends, because who wants to associate with someone married to a woman like that? He might have even lost his authority as God's spokesman, because what man of God would marry a sinful woman? He accepted the pain because he knew it was God's plan.

In this way, Hosea was a lot like Jesus, whom we talked about a few days ago. Even as Jesus asked God if there was another way, He said "Not as I will, but as you will." (Matthew 26:39) Hosea did the same thing when he married a woman he knew would bring him heartache.

If I'm completely honest, I don't know if I would have been able to do what Hosea did. I am all for God's plan when it is something that makes me happy. That is why those preachers are so popular. It's nice to think of God smiling as we smile and cheering as things go well in our lives.

But I can't ignore the books in the Bible that teach otherwise, books like Hosea that remind us God's plan can be painful at times. In Ezekiel we are told that God allowed Ezekiel's wife to die as an object lesson for the people of Israel, and the entire book of Jeremiah describes how the people tried to kill the prophet just because he chose to speak the Words of the Lord.

These stories, and others throughout the Bible, prove God's plan doesn't always add up to an easy one. They also force us to ask an important question. Are we willing to follow God's plan even if it hurts?

Jesus urged His followers to count the cost of following Him. At times, that cost might be painful, but I can promise you, it's always worth it.

QUESTIONS FOR REFLECTION

1. Do you agree or disagree that God wants us to be happy? Explain your answer.
2. Why do you think God sometimes asks us to do things that are painful?

PRAYER

Pray for God to build your faith and trust in Him so much you are willing to follow Him and obey Him, even if what He asks of you is painful.

SCRIPTURES FOR FURTHER MEDITATION

Matthew 26:36–46, Ezekiel 24:15–18, Luke 14:25–33

JOURNAL ACTIVITY

Find the song "Praise You in the Storm" by Casting Crowns on YouTube. As you listen to the song, write in your journal some of the words that speak to you.

TAKEAWAY

When bad things happen to good people, obey God anyway.

John the Baptist

Scripture reading: Matthew 11:1–5

"When John, who was in prison, heard about the deeds of the Messiah, he sent his disciples to ask him, 'Are you the one who is to come, or should we expect someone else?'" — Matthew 11:2–3

A few weeks ago, I went to a conference for moms. While there, I attended a class about when and how to talk to your children about sex. My children are five and two, but I wanted to get a head start on this very important topic.

Leaving that class, I had one goal in mind... to make certain I did everything in my power to encourage my kids to come to me or my husband with their questions instead of going to their friends.

Even if my boys have the greatest of friends, I don't want them asking friends advice on issues like this because kids don't know enough about God's design for sex to teach anyone else. My husband and I, on the other hand, know the truth. We are more than happy, though admittedly a little nervous, to share the truth with our kids.

I think God feels the same way about our questions. He wants us to come to Him instead of looking to the world for answers. We aren't supposed to turn to our friends or to books first, though He often uses both of these to help us understand Him. We are supposed to turn to Him before anyone else. Before we ask Siri on our phones or Google on our computers, He longs for us to come to Him with our questions.

That's exactly what John the Baptist did. Even before he was born, he recognized Jesus as God's Holy One. When a pregnant Elizabeth greeted a pregnant Mary, John "leaped" in Elizabeth's womb (Luke 1:41) because he recognized Jesus as God's Son. Years later, as adults, when Jesus came to John to be baptized, John hesitated because he felt unworthy to baptize the Son of God. "I need to be baptized by you," John told Jesus in Matthew 3:14. John witnessed God's Holy Spirit come upon Jesus after His baptism. John knew — without a doubt — Jesus was the One for whom everyone had been waiting. In John 1:34, he said, "I have seen and I testify that this is God's Chosen One."

John knew Jesus was the Savior, but then life happened, and he began to doubt. Maybe your story is similar. Mine is. I didn't grow up in the church. I chose to follow Jesus as my Lord and Savior as a teenager. When I first became a disciple, I was on fire for the Lord. I wanted to learn all I could about Jesus. I feasted on the Bible and couldn't get enough of it. Then, after high school, I enrolled in Bible college and spent hundreds of hours learning about Jesus, God, and the Bible.

After I graduated, I thought I knew Jesus pretty well. My faith was strong, but then life got difficult, and doubts began to seep into my soul. Maybe I was wrong and God wasn't really who I thought He was.

This is what happened to John the Baptist. He knew who Jesus was, but when Herod threw John the Baptist in prison, he started to question the things he knew. There, in his cold, blackened cell, doubts began to creep in. *Maybe Jesus isn't the one. Maybe I was wrong when I thought I saw the Holy Spirit coming upon him.* He sent men to ask Jesus, "Are you the one who is to come, or should we expect someone else?" (Matthew 11:3)

Jesus told the men to tell John what they saw — Jesus healing people and preaching the good news. Then He said to those listening, "Truly I tell you, among those born of women there has not risen anyone greater than John the Baptist." (Matthew 11:11) This is *so* significant! Even though John had just expressed doubts, Jesus still praised him as great.

For some reason, many of us assume good Christians don't have doubts and that Jesus isn't comfortable with our questions, but John's story proves otherwise. He was someone Jesus said was one of the greatest people who ever lived, yet John doubted when life got hard. Doubt isn't sin. What is wrong is refusing to come to Jesus with those doubts.

John the Baptist left us an example to follow. When he doubted, he came to Jesus with his questions. He didn't stuff his doubts deep in his heart, hoping they would go away. He didn't look to those around him for answers. Instead, he went straight to the Source for His answer.

What's amazing is that you and I can do the same thing. Because of Jesus' sacrifice on the cross, we have access to the Source of answers too. The question is, will we run to Him with our doubts, or will we seek our answers elsewhere?

QUESTIONS FOR REFLECTION

1. Whom do you often turn to when you have questions about your faith? If not God, why?
2. Why is it important to run to God first with our questions?

PRAYER

Ask God to give you the courage to run to Him with your questions about faith and prompt your spirit to ask Him before you do anything else.

SCRIPTURES FOR FURTHER MEDITATION

Jude 1:22, Matthew 14:22–31, Luke 24:36–43, Mark 9:14–29

JOURNAL ACTIVITY

In your journal, make a list of some of your questions for God (e.g., why do bad things happen to good people? Why is the Old Testament full of violence? Etc.). Then bring each of these questions to the Lord. He might not answer all of them right now; however, if you pray over this list and then search His word, He will either answer your questions or help you come to peace with the unknown.

TAKEAWAY

When bad things happen to good people, come to Jesus with your doubts.

When You Are Stuck in the Shadows

Kids love shadows. My two-year-old works hard to catch his. Something happens, though, when we grow up. Most adults don't like shadows anymore. They are scary and full of danger. We avoid them when we take an early morning run or walk down an unfamiliar street.

We avoid metaphorical ones too. We don't like it when no one notices us or when we get excluded from a friend's plans. We don't like feeling unknown or insignificant.

This week, we'll look at six biblical men and women who were stuck in metaphorical shadows. Some of them, like Rachel, Leah, and Hagar, for example, could have easily battled feelings of insecurity or worthlessness. Others, like John the Baptist and David, had to learn to give up the spotlight for a greater cause. Joshua, in a similar fashion, could have easily battled feelings of self-doubt because his predecessor, Moses, cast such a long shadow.

We're going to learn what to do when it seems no one notices us, when we feel worthless, and when we wonder if we're doing anything that matters. We'll also discuss some of the benefits of being an unknown individual in a world that values fame.

After you complete this week's lessons, please watch the video at...

www.crossrivermedia.com/portfolio/unbeaten-week-six

Rachel and Leah

Scripture reading: Genesis 29:13–30:24

Jacob's *"love for Rachel was greater than his love for Leah...When the* LORD *saw that Leah was not loved, he enabled her to conceive, but Rachel remained childless."* — Genesis 29:30–31

We live in a Pintastic world. I love Pinterest, Facebook, and social media just as much as anyone else, but sometimes it makes it hard to feel like I'm enough. We garner our self-esteem based on how many Facebook friends we have. If people like, comment, or share our posts, we feel good about ourselves. But what about when no one likes our posts? What about when no one retweets us?

If our self-esteem is based on the reactions of other people on social media, we are certain to be disappointed often. What's worse, if our self-esteem rises and falls with social media, we are bound to get caught in the comparison game. Steven Furtick said, "The reason we struggle with insecurity is because we compare our behind-the-scenes with everyone else's highlight reel."[1]

We notice a friend's photo album with vacation photos and assume her family has more fun than we do. We see a picture of a dozen roses with a card that reads "Just Because" on someone's Facebook wall and assume her marriage must be better than ours. It's so easy, while browsing through our newsfeeds, to lose sight of the blessings in our lives because we are wishing for the blessings in another's.

This problem isn't new to us, though. Granted, social media has added a new element to insecurity. But feeling less than has been a struggle for decades. Today, let's look at Rachel and Leah.

Rachel and Leah were the two wives of Jacob, and they were sisters.

Both of them had an understandable reason to feel insecure. Leah was the lesser loved of the two sisters. The only reason Jacob even married her was because her father tricked him into it. From her perspective, it would be easy to assume she would never be pretty enough to gain the love of her husband. He had eyes for one woman, and that woman was her sister. Day after day, I imagine Leah tried to make herself look more beautiful, but her efforts failed. Every. Single. Time. Jacob loved Rachel... period.

On the flip side, though, Rachel also had good reason to feel insecure. She couldn't have children. In our culture today, infertility is devastating. It can wreck marriages, finances, faith, friendships, and just about every area of a person's life.

In Rachel's culture, it was even worse. Not only did she have to deal with the anguish of not being able to birth a child, she also had to deal with the teaching that barrenness was a curse from God. From her perspective, Rachel may have felt her sister was the lucky one. Leah could do something for Jacob Rachel couldn't do: provide him with children and give him the legacy he needed. Rachel might have been the pretty one, but she wasn't the blessed one, at least not from her perspective.

Both women had understandable reasons for insecurity. One, no matter how hard she tried, could never be as loved as the other. The other, no matter how much she prayed, could never get her body to work as her sister's did. The rivalry became so fierce both women eventually gave their servants to Jacob, in hopes of claiming their servants' children as their own. (You can read all about the rivalry in Genesis 30.)

Both Rachel and Leah failed to see themselves through God's eyes. Unfortunately, we still struggle with this today. We see the things we can't do when God sees the things we can. We see our failures when God sees our successes. We see our imperfections; God sees our beauty. We see all the things that label us not enough when God sees His children, whom He adores more than anything else in this world.

Jennifer Dukes Lee, in her book *Love Idol*, says, "Christians sing of God's love beneath wooden crosses on Sundays, but we go looking for love and approval in all the wrong places the other six days of the week."[2]

Is this true for you? Do you claim to believe God loves you but still look for love elsewhere? Maybe you look for it in a relationship or in a bottle. Maybe you search for it online.

Can I challenge you with something? When you're feeling less than, don't look to social media or to a person for your affirmation. Look to God. When you're feeling not enough, don't try to make yourself better. Look to the One who has already made you white as snow.

QUESTIONS FOR REFLECTION

1. In what area of your life do you struggle with insecurity?
2. Why do you think insecurity is such a problem, specifically among women?

PRAYER

Pray for God to help you see yourself as He sees you. He doesn't see you as less than or as a failure. He sees you as enough. Ask for His eyes.

SCRIPTURES FOR FURTHER MEDITATION

Psalm 139:13–14, Genesis 1:27, Isaiah 43:1

JOURNAL ACTIVITY

Look back at Week 2, Day 1, the devotional on Esther. For your journal activity that day, you listed some of the names God has given you in His Word. Today, look up one more verse: Zephaniah 3:17. Write in your journal what this verse says God thinks about you.

TAKEAWAY

When you're stuck in the shadows, find your worth through God's eyes.

DAY TWO

Joshua

Scripture reading: Joshua 1:1–9

"Be strong and very courageous. Be careful to obey all the law my servant Moses gave you; do not turn from it to the right or to the left, that you may be successful wherever you go." — Joshua 1:7

H ave you ever wondered why racehorses wear those things around their eyes? Last summer, my children and I watched the movie *Racing Stripes* about a zebra that believed he was a racehorse. After the movie ended, my kids asked me why Stripes, the zebra, wore patches on his eyes. I investigated online and learned these patches are called blinkers or blinders.

Many trainers believe blinders block out distractions and help the horses focus only on the track before them. There are many potential distractions for racehorses — the crowd, the other horses, and a variety of other nature sounds. It makes sense trainers would want to keep these distractions at a minimum. Blinders are a great way to do it.

Like racehorses, we too have a lot of distractions vying for our attention and trying to keep us from living the lives God longs us to live. One huge distraction is of our own making. It's our insecurity. For some reason, even though the Word of God is abundantly clear we are beautiful, amazing, children of God, we forget.

Just as horses get distracted when they see other racers, we get distracted when we fix our eyes on other people. As a teenager, one of my best friends was a girl by the same name as me. For some reason, I never felt confident when I was around her. Even though I was small, I felt fat. Even though I was far from ugly, I felt ugly when I was around her. Some people, oblivious to how much their words hurt, referred to her as the little Lindsey. Of course, when I heard this description, I assumed that made me the big Lindsey. It wasn't true, but that's what happens when we fix our eyes on those around us. We see their successes and our failures. Their beauty and our flaws.

Comparing ourselves to other people does nothing but distract us from the joy God longs for us to have. Comparisons also distract us from our callings.

As a writer, there are plenty of successful authors I could easily compare myself to. When I compare, though, the questions and doubts begin to surface: Maybe I'm not good at this after all. Why isn't my book selling well on Amazon? Maybe God didn't call me to write.

When I fix my eyes on others, I stop trying to be faithful to God and start trying to be successful to the world. Or, worse yet, I stop trying at all. I quit because I don't think I can do it.

Joshua, in our text for today, could have easily struggled with comparisons. After all, he followed in the footsteps of Moses, the man whom the Bible says spoke with God face to face. (Exodus 33:11) It's understandable why Joshua might have felt inadequate.

God didn't let Joshua throw himself a pity party and focus on his insecurity, though. Instead, God armed Joshua with a strategy. In Joshua 1:7, God told him, "Be strong and very courageous. Be careful to obey all the law my servant Moses gave you; do not turn from it to the right or to the left, that you may be successful wherever you go." In essence, God said to him, "Put your blinders on and focus on Me and on My Word." He told him to not turn from it to the right or to the left.

I wonder how our lives would change if we, too, stopped looking at the people around us and focused, instead, on God's Word and on God's calling in our lives. Joshua, later on in his ministry, said these words, "But as for me and my household, we will serve the LORD." (Joshua 24:15) Based on this text, I think Joshua finally learned to live with blinders on. He learned how to focus — not on his failures or on others' successes — but on his calling and on the One who called him.

This made all the difference for Joshua, and it'll make all the difference for us, too. Put on your blinders today, friends, and fix your eyes on Jesus for the race. Putting on blinders means filling your mind each day with God's Word. It means paying attention to where your thoughts are wandering and redirecting them to things that are true, noble, right, pure, lovely, and admirable. (Philippians 4:8) It means avoiding people or places that hinder your walk with the Lord and surrounding yourself with only those things that help you fix your eyes on Jesus. And it means avoiding the comparison trap.

I love what Hebrews 12:1–2 says: "Let us throw off everything that hinders and the sin that so easily entangles. And let us run with perseverance the race marked out for us, fixing our eyes on Jesus." Instead of focusing on those running beside us, let's focus on the One at the finish line.

QUESTIONS FOR REFLECTION

1. In what area of your life do you struggle with comparisons (e.g., your abilities, your marriage, your parenting, your work, etc.)?
2. How do you think Joshua felt as he followed in the footsteps of Moses? How would you have felt?

PRAYER

Ask God to help you keep your eyes on Him. Pray for a singular focus, that you won't compare yourself with others but will gaze instead on the One who called you.

SCRIPTURES FOR FURTHER MEDITATION

1 Samuel 16:1–13, Matthew 10:29–31, Zephaniah 3:17

JOURNAL ACTIVITY

When I was in college and struggling with insecurity, my older brother challenged me to write three things per day I liked about myself. It wasn't an exercise in pride; rather, it was an exercise in learning to thank God for the gifts, talents, and blessings He gave me. Write three things in your journal you believe God has blessed you with. These could be personality traits, abilities, strengths, etc.

TAKEAWAY

When you're stuck in the shadows, stop comparing yourself to others. Instead, fix your eyes on your Father.

John the Baptist

Scripture reading: John 3:22–30

*"He must become greater;
I must become less." — John 3:30*

One of my favorite Christian bands is Shane and Shane. I love their music because of the way the voices of Shane Barnard and Shane Everett blend with one another. I am not a music expert, but I do know music sounds amazing when tenor notes blend with bass or baritone notes.

Likewise, someone singing harmony might not sound beautiful if you only listened to her. But, open your ears to the melody, and an amazing thing happens. Harmony and melody blend together in such a way that art is formed. This art changes lives, melts hearts, and sometimes even creates goose bumps on the arms of those listening.

The reality about music is that it wouldn't sound as lovely if there were no harmony. It also wouldn't sound as beautiful if there were no backup singers. Backup singers might not feel as important as lead singers, but they are. In a band, there are guitar players, vocalists, drummers, pianists, and a variety of other musicians. Some of these might not sound great alone, but when they are joined with others, create a song that has the power to change lives.

This is also true in the Christian world. Sometimes, if we're not speaking from a platform or making a difference among thousands of people, we are tempted to feel like we don't matter. Maybe you're a stay-at-home mom who often wonders if she's influencing anyone for Jesus. Let me reassure you, you are. You are influencing those little ones more than anyone else. Who knows what they might grow up to do someday? You might be the one who influences the one who changes the world.

Or maybe you work in an office. You spend most of your day filing papers and wonder: How is filing papers making a difference in anyone's life? Maybe you work at a grocery store, bagging groceries. Whatever you do, whether you work with only one or with thousands of people, you are making a difference. Your life does matter. That smile you offer to a stranger, that prayer you lift to God for a coworker, that kind word you utter to a child, all of these things make a difference. You might be working in the shadows, but you are shining your light on Jesus.

In today's get famous quick culture, in which someone can be famous instantly via Facebook or YouTube, living in the shadows can be difficult. Feeling like you have nothing to offer, nothing that is tweet-worthy, can wear down even the most confident person.

But here's the truth — even if you never say anything that gets shared on Twitter, even if you never write a best-selling book, even if you never get your name listed in the newspaper, your small actions are worthy of applause. Someday, Jesus is going to give you that applause. That, my friends, is a much better reward than this world's praise.

One biblical figure who understood what it felt like to live in the shadows was John the Baptist. His ministry, that had once been successful and growing, was beginning to shrink as Jesus' ministry grew. Even some of John's own followers were deserting him to follow Jesus.

It would have been easy for John to grow discouraged or jealous. He might have been tempted to prevent anyone else from leaving him by speaking negatively about Jesus. What's amazing is, John didn't do that. In fact, he did the opposite. He encouraged them to leave. In John 3:30, he said, "He must become greater; I must become less." He understood his role in this life much better than many of us do today.

Our purpose is not to make a name for ourselves — it is to make a name for Jesus. We shouldn't try to get out of the shadows and stand in the limelight. We are to shine our lights on our Lord, regardless of whether we are known by many or by few.

Our culture might try to convince us we are nothing if we're not in the limelight, but John the Baptist proves otherwise. Being in the shadows is often the best place to be. Where else but in the dark can we shine such a bright light on our Lord?

QUESTIONS FOR REFLECTION

1. What is the most difficult aspect of being unknown?
2. Do you think there is anything wrong with being famous as a Christian? Why or why not? What are some of the dangers of fame among Christians?

PRAYER

Pray for God to give you contentment in the shadows. Also pray that if you ever do become a well-known Christian, that you will care more about making Jesus known than making yourself known.

SCRIPTURES FOR FURTHER MEDITATION

Colossians 3:23, Ephesians 2:10

JOURNAL ACTIVITY

John 3:30 should be the goal of every believer. Our job is to make Jesus more and ourselves less. Write this verse in your journal and then commit it to memory over the next few days. "He must become greater; I must become less."

TAKEAWAY

When you're stuck in the shadows, shine your light on Jesus.

David

Scripture reading: 1 Samuel 16:1–23

"Then the Lord said, 'Rise and anoint him;
this is the one.'" — 1 Samuel 16:12

One of the most difficult aspects of being a writer is when no one reads what I've written.

I once wrote what I thought was a great post. Before you assume that's the norm, let me reassure you. Like most writers, I struggle to believe I can write at all most days. But this post was different. I thought *for sure* it would be repinned and shared several times. Instead, it just sat there with no comments or shares. Nothing.

Have you ever been there? You know God has big plans for your life, and you work hard, but months or even years go by without the success you thought God would grant you.

If you're a musician, maybe no one buys your music or comes to your shows. As a minister, maybe your church seems stagnant. You've worked your tail off only to see the same fifty faces every single Sunday. You love those people but wonder why more aren't coming. Or at home, you try to be a good mother and wife, but your kids don't behave or your husband feels more distant now than he did a month ago.

What do you do when you're in the shadows and success seems out of reach, when you wonder if what you're doing day after day even matters?

That's the question I believe David asked himself many times. After all, in 1 Samuel 16, God promised David he would be king. After the prophet Samuel traveled to David's home, God said about David, "'Rise and anoint him; this is the one.' So Samuel took the horn of oil and anointed him in the presence of his brothers, and from that day on the Spirit of the Lord came powerfully upon David." (1 Samuel 16:12-13)

Even though Samuel anointed David as king and even though the Spirit of the Lord came upon him, David's life didn't change for quite awhile. He continued to be a shepherd. He spent some time in the king's home, playing music to soothe Saul, but nothing else changed. David served the king rather than became one. God promised a kingdom; David got a life of mediocrity, at least for a while.

Eventually, God did fulfill His promise, but it wasn't until after a long and painful season of running from King Saul. David was successful in the end, but that success followed pain that many of us cannot fathom. The light came, but only after a long walk through the dark.

We might feel as though God has led us to something great. The question is, are we willing to wait until He fulfills His promise? Are we willing to remain in the shadows until He's ready for us to succeed? And, most importantly, are we willing to accept His definition of success, even if it differs from the world's definition?

To the world, success means popularity and money. God's definition of success is different. To Him, success is faithfulness. That dedication might lead to prestige or monetary gain, or it might not. To the world, success is fame. To God, it's faithfulness.

In the parable of the talents in Matthew 25, Jesus told the story of three servants. One servant was given five talents, one was given two, and one was given one. The servants who were given five and two talents were faithful with theirs. Their master rewarded them for their hard work. The servant with one, on the other hand, did nothing with his talent. When the master returned, he reprimanded the lazy servant.

What's interesting about this text is that Jesus didn't focus on the size of the harvest with any of the servants. Instead, he put the focus on the servants' faithfulness. "Well done, good and faithful servant! You have been faithful with a few things." (Matthew 25:21) What this teaches us is that God isn't as concerned with the size of our return as He is with our faithfulness. To Him, faithfulness is what matters. Not fame.

After my blog post didn't take off, God reminded me it can be good to be in the shadows. Being an instant success might not be all we'd hoped it would be. Success puts us in the spotlight. If we make a mistake, there are plenty of people to make sure we don't forget it. On the other hand, if we make our mistakes now, while there are only a few people watching, the fallout won't be as large.

There's another reason too… being in the shadows allows the spotlight to shine on Jesus. As we are faithful in the shadows, God gets the glory. That, my friends, is a pretty good reason to be content right where we are, even if no one outside of our hometown knows our name.

QUESTIONS FOR REFLECTION

1. Why do you think God didn't make David king immediately? Do you think there was a reason for the wait?
2. What are some of the benefits of being in the shadows?
3. In what do you hope God gives you success? (e.g., writing, parenting, work, teaching, music, ministry, etc.)

PRAYER

Thank God He chose to live in the shadows. Thank Him for leaving His glorious throne for the dirty streets of Earth. Ask Him to help you be faithful in the shadows so He gets the glory He deserves.

SCRIPTURES FOR FURTHER MEDITATION

Philippians 2:5–7, Matthew 20:20–28

JOURNAL ACTIVITY

Draw a picture of a candle in darkness, then below it write this Edith Wharton quote: "There are two ways of spreading light: to be the candle or the mirror that reflects it." Write ways you reflect Jesus in your life.

TAKEAWAY

When you're stuck in the shadows, be content where you are.

Hagar

Scripture reading: Genesis 16:1–16

"She gave this name to the LORD who spoke to her: 'You are the God who sees me.'" — *Genesis 16:13*

We all want to be seen.

If you don't believe me, spend the day with a toddler. This morning, my two-year-old son discovered that when he swallowed a drink of milk, his neck moved. To an adult, this might not be too impressive, but to him, it was amazing. He was so excited he ran over to me, grabbed my hand, and pulled me to the table where his sippy cup sat. "Watch, Mommy, watch!"

He threw his head back and gulped down more milk to show me how his neck moved, then checked to make sure I watched the entire event. I had, of course, because I know how important it is for children to feel seen.

This desire to be seen never really goes away. Sure, we might hide it as adults. We pretend it doesn't bother us when someone forgets to invite us to a get-together. We say it's no big deal when we are left out or forgotten, but deep down, we all want to be seen. That child who longs for his mother to come and watch him never really outgrows his need to be noticed.

What I love about today's text is the reminder that God sees us. Even if everyone else forgets about us, He is the God who sees. I'm getting ahead of myself, though. Let's take a look at Hagar's story.

Hagar was Sarai's slave — the same Sarai who later changed her name to Sarah, wife of Abraham. Life was hard for Hagar. She most likely had very few freedoms. Then, in Genesis 16, Sarai forced Hagar to sleep with Abram to provide children for Sarai. In those days, if a woman could not conceive, she could claim the children of her slave as her own. This is exactly what Sarai planned to do. Unfortunately, when

Hagar became pregnant, tensions grew between the two women, and Sarai mistreated Hagar.

Put yourself in Hagar's shoes for a moment. She was a slave, pregnant and likely hormonal and uncomfortable. To make matters worse, she was mistreated — not for doing anything wrong but because she obeyed her master. Finally, Hagar had enough and ran away from Abram and Sarai, hoping to escape her problems.

There, in the desert, as she sat alone and rejected, an angel of the Lord found Hagar and comforted her when she needed it most. A little later, in Genesis 16:13, Hagar named the One who came to her: "You are the God who sees me." I love this text for two reasons.

First of all, it says the angel of the Lord found Hagar. I imagine the angel doing everything in His power to meet her in her time of need. It reminds me of the story of the lost sheep in Luke 15. The shepherd desperately searched for that lost sheep until he found it, and then carried it home on his shoulders. He even left his ninety-nine other sheep behind because of how much he loved the one lost sheep. In this text in Genesis, Hagar was the lost sheep, and God would stop at nothing to find her.

A second thing I love is God saw Hagar at her worst and lifted her from despair. All too often, when you or I see someone suffering, we look away in discomfort. If we see a homeless man asking for money at a stoplight, we pray the light changes quickly. If we see someone crying at church, we look away for fear she'd be embarrassed of her tears. But God doesn't do that. He doesn't look away from suffering. He looks toward it. He searches for the hurting, the poor, and the broken. He sees them — really sees them — for the men and women they are.

Psalm 34:15–18 says, "The eyes of the LORD are on the righteous, and his ears are attentive to their cry;… The righteous cry out, and the LORD hears them; he delivers them from all their troubles. The LORD is close to the brokenhearted and saves those who are crushed in spirit."

Today, if you are wondering if anyone sees you, rest in the knowledge there is a God who sees. Better yet, rest in the knowledge there is a God who sees *and* who comes to your rescue. His eyes are on you, His ears are attentive, and His hands are open to catch your tears as they slide off your cheeks.

QUESTIONS FOR REFLECTION

1. How do you think Hagar felt before God found her in the desert?
2. Have you ever longed for someone to truly see and love you as you are?
3. How does it make you feel to realize God not only sees you, but also searches for ways to bring you into His loving embrace?

PRAYER

Thank God He is "the God who sees." Even when others might not notice you, He always will.

SCRIPTURES FOR MEDITATION

Psalm 34:15–18, John 10:14, 1 John 5:14, 1 Peter 3:12

JOURNAL ACTIVITY

Draw something in your journal as a reminder God always sees you. It could be a picture of an eye or sunglasses. Use your imagination. Then write beside your picture "I am seen."

TAKEAWAY

When you're stuck in the shadows, remember God sees you.

When You Did Nothing Wrong

Sometimes, we can legitimately blame ourselves for bad things that happen to us. We get exactly what we deserve. This will be the theme for next week's devotionals. Other times, though, we do everything right and still face tragedy.

Throughout the next five days, we're going to study the lives of several biblical figures who seemed to have chosen the short straw with their lives. Those around them, sometimes even those who were living sinful lifestyles, prospered while they suffered. Esau, for instance, was betrayed by his brother, Jacob. He lost his blessing through no fault of his own. We'll study his life to learn about forgiveness.

We'll also look at the lives of Joseph, Jesus, Peter, and Elijah. Each of their stories will remind us that suffering isn't reserved for the wicked. Bad things do, in fact, happen to good people. This week, we'll answer the question, what do you do when life goes south because of no fault of your own?

After you complete this week's lessons, please watch the video at...

www.crossrivermedia.com/portfolio/unbeaten-week-seven

Esau

Scripture reading: Genesis 27:1–41 and Genesis 33

*"The Lᴏʀᴅ said to her, 'Two nations are in your womb, and
two peoples from within you will be separated;
one people will be stronger than the other, and the older
will serve the younger.'" — Genesis 25:23*

Months before my husband and I even discussed having a second child, I began taking prenatal vitamins. I wanted to make sure my body was as healthy as possible for a baby. I didn't smoke, drink, or use drugs. I exercised regularly, but not so hard it would hurt a baby in utero.

Why, then, didn't our pregnancies progress? Other women, who might have done all of the harmful things I didn't, had no problem carrying a baby to term. They might have even done these things while pregnant without any complications. If I am completely honest, I feel short-changed at times. I deserve the blessing of a child.

Have you ever been there? You might not admit it aloud, but maybe you feel like you've lived a pretty good life. You don't participate in some of the sinful behaviors your coworkers do. You go to church every Sunday. You try your best to live for Jesus throughout the week. So why isn't God blessing you for your faithfulness? Why does it seem He is blessing others, even if they don't seem to deserve the blessings?

Today, we're going to look at a man who didn't receive some of the blessings he deserved. This man's name was Esau. Esau was far from perfect, as you'll see if you dig into Genesis 25–28. Nonetheless, I feel bad for the guy. Even though he was the firstborn son of Isaac and Rebecca, he didn't receive any of the privileges of being the firstborn because his brother took them from him. Granted, part of the reason he lost some of his firstborn privileges was his own fault — when he traded his birthright for a bowl of soup. Still, even though his birthright was lost because of his bad decision, his blessing was lost because of his brother's deceit.

Esau deserved the blessing from his father. It was his right as the firstborn son. The only reason he didn't receive it was because his little brother tricked their dad. Jacob covered himself with goatskin so his arms felt hairy like his brother's. He put on some of Esau's clothing to make himself smell like his older sibling. Then he brought food in to his aged father, lied about his identity, and stole the blessing that was rightfully Esau's. (You can read the entire story in Genesis 27.)

Can you blame Esau for being angry, for feeling short-changed, cheated, and deceived? I imagine I would have felt the same way. What's amazing, though, is that Esau forgave Jacob.

In Genesis 33, after the brothers had been apart for many years, Jacob returned home. While on the way, Jacob looked up and saw Esau coming toward him with 400 men. Understandably, Jacob was afraid of what Esau might do to him and his family. Jacob ran toward Esau and bowed before him seven times. In that moment, when Esau had good reason to seek revenge from his lying, cheating brother, he instead embraced him, threw his arms around his neck, and kissed him. (Genesis 33:4) When Jacob offered gifts to Esau as a peace offering, Esau reassured Jacob all was forgiven.

Esau could have hung onto his bitterness and anger, but he forgave instead. I read this quote from Jennifer Rothschild recently: "You may have the right to be angry, but is it a right worth exercising?"[1] Esau had a right to hang on to his anger toward Jacob, but he chose not to exercise that right.

You and I have a choice, too, when other people hurt us and for times when we feel God has let us down. Is it possible you're mad at God for allowing whatever painful event brought you to this devotional? Holding on to anger isn't doing you any good. Letting go, on the other hand, and choosing to give up that right brings freedom.

About six months ago, my church did a series on forgiveness. On the last week of the series, as I walked into our auditorium, I saw a black coffin at the front of the stage. When services began, our minister passed out pieces of paper to everyone and asked us to each write the names of people we needed to forgive. He then challenged us to put the names in the coffin as a visual representation of burying the unforgiveness.

As I slowly wrote the letters G-O-D and then folded my paper and placed it in the coffin, I felt something I hadn't felt in years — freedom.

Max Lucado says "forgiveness is unlocking the door to set someone free and realizing you were that prisoner." Anger and bitterness might be understandable in your situation. You might be able to rightfully claim those as yours. If you do, you'll never experience true freedom. Can I challenge you to forgive? If God let you down, forgive Him. If your spouse broke your heart, forgive him. They might not deserve your forgiveness, but you deserve freedom, and freedom is only found in forgiveness.

QUESTIONS FOR REFLECTION

1. When have you felt short-changed, either by God or by someone else?
2. Do you believe you have the right to be angry? Why or why not? Is it a right worth exercising?

PRAYER

Ask God to help you forgive those in your life who have taken advantage of you. If God was the One who short-changed you, tell Him about it and ask Him to help you forgive.

SCRIPTURES FOR FURTHER MEDITATION

Matthew 6:14–15, Mark 11:25, Ephesians 4:31–32, Romans 12:19

JOURNAL ACTIVITY

Whom in your life do you need to forgive? Write each name in your journal and then pray over your list, asking God to help you forgive.

TAKEAWAY

When you did nothing wrong, forgive those who did.

Joseph

Scripture reading: Genesis 50:15–21

*"You intended to harm me, but God intended it
for good to accomplish what is now being done,
the saving of many lives."* — *Genesis 50:20*

Not long ago, I took my two sons on a nature walk around the neighborhood. They are five and two. We weren't two steps from our house when my five-year-old insisted we stop and look at the beautiful flower at his feet.

I love a beautiful flower as much as anyone, but this flower wasn't even a flower. It was a weed. As I garnered up all the excitement I could manage and bent down to inspect his find, I remembered something I read recently about choosing to look for the flowers among the weeds. I was immediately convicted because all I saw was a pesky weed, whereas my son found the flower.

You've probably heard someone say there are two kinds of people in the world — half-full and half-empty people. There are some who think of the glass as half-full. These are your optimists. Then there are others who are half-empty people, your Negative Nancys and your weed-finders. Sometimes I am a half-empty kind of girl.

Our biblical figure today is not. He's a half-full kind of person, someone who can find the bright spot in even the darkest of nights. Joseph was really good at finding the flowers among the weeds.

We talked about Joseph's faithfulness when faced with temptation in Week Five. This week, I want to look at his relationship with his brothers. Joseph was one of Jacob's twelve sons. In fact, he was Jacob's favorite. Because Jacob favored Joseph so much, the other brothers grew more and more hostile toward him. They despised their brother so much that one day, they sold him into slavery and told his father a wild animal killed him.

The brothers' lives went on as they had before, but Joseph's kept getting worse and worse. Every time he thought he might finally catch a break, something went wrong and sent him spiraling.

Others would have been bitter toward the brothers, but not Joseph. He had the power to pay back his brothers for the evil they did to him, but chose to forgive them and offer grace.

Here's how it happened. After Joseph's brothers sold him into slavery, Joseph worked for a time in the home of Potiphar, the captain of the palace guard. Then, because of a false accusation, Joseph was sent to prison. Years later, God brought Joseph out of prison and enabled him to become second in command in Egypt. During this time, a famine struck the whole land, and Joseph's brothers came to Egypt in search of food. Now a man of power, Joseph had the perfect chance to pay them back for what they did to him, but he didn't. He chose to forgive when he could have punished.

Romans 8:28 says, "And we know that in all things God works for the good of those who love him, who have been called according to his purpose." Joseph never heard this verse, but that didn't matter. He lived it. He understood, more than most, that God can bring good from any situation.

Did you notice that it says in all things? It doesn't say God works in most things or in nearly all things or in the good things. It says *all*. That means God can work in a divorce. He can work in a health crisis. He can work in cancer. He can work in joblessness. He can work in infertility. He can even work in death. There is *no* circumstance through which God cannot work.

Joseph never read this Bible verse, but he understood its truth. He knew God was with him, working in and through every difficult situation he faced, to bring about the deliverance of the Jewish nation. While some might have sought revenge, Joseph offered grace, because he saw God's hand in it all. He, just like my son on our nature walk, looked for the flowers among the weeds.

Psalm 112:4 says, "Even in darkness light dawns for the upright." It

123

wasn't that Joseph had no darkness in his life; it was that he was able to find the light even when there was little light to find.

QUESTIONS FOR REFLECTION

1. What are some of the flowers in your negative situation?
2. What helps you focus on the positive aspects of your life, especially when the negative aspects are easier to see?
3. What other character qualities do you think Joseph had that helped him forgive his brothers?

PRAYER

Pray for God to bring good from your hard situation. Ask Him to help you find the flowers among the weeds.

SCRIPTURES FOR FURTHER MEDITATION

Romans 8:28, Psalm 112:4, Philippians 4:8

JOURNAL ACTIVITY

It's easy to fixate on the negative and miss the positive. Flip to about halfway through your journal and write at the top of that page, "Gratitude Journal." Each night before bed, write at least one thing for which you are grateful. Continue doing this throughout the rest of the weeks as you work through this devotional.

TAKEAWAY

When you did nothing wrong, look for the flowers among the weeds.

Elijah

Scripture reading: 1 Kings 18:16–19:8

*"'I have had enough, Lord,' he said. 'Take my life;
I am no better than my ancestors.'" — 1 Kings 19:4*

My husband is one of those people who never gets sick. I could probably cough into his mouth, and his amazing immune system would fight off those germs in hours. It's disgusting, I know, but also true. I, on the other hand, am almost guaranteed to get sick when I'm around someone with a cold. If my children are sick one day, you can bet I'll catch it the next.

Immunity against sickness is one thing. Immunity against suffering and doubt is another. Though some of us might have better chances of fighting off the flu, all of us have an equal chance of experiencing pain. In fact, it's guaranteed. In James 1:2–3, the brother of Jesus wrote, "Consider it pure joy, my brothers and sisters, whenever you face trials of many kinds, because you know that the testing of your faith produces perseverance." James didn't say *if* you face trials, but *when* you face them. Difficulties are just a part of life. No one is immune to them.

Sometimes, even though we know everyone struggles and most have doubts, we have a hard time convincing our hearts it's true. I know in my head even the strongest Christians doubt God from time to time, but when I doubt Him, I feel guilty. How could a believer in Jesus, and a minister's wife at that, doubt the One I claim to follow? How could someone who has given her life to God wonder at times if He really loves her?

One thing that encourages me is when I dig into the pages of God's Word, I find most of the heroes of the faith doubted God at times too. One such example is Elijah. Elijah was one of the most famous prophets in the Old Testament. He heard from God on a regular basis, but even he doubted God's love for him.

The part of his story I want to focus on today is in 1 Kings 19, but let's back up to read the context. In 1 Kings 18, Elijah went before the evil King Ahab and challenged 450 prophets of the idol Baal. The 450 prophets prayed for Baal to send fire on their offering, and Elijah prayed for God to do the same on his. In an amazing show of power, the Lord sent fire that not only burned the sacrifice, but also the wood, stones, soil, and water around the altar. The people watching killed all 450 prophets of Baal because they realized the Lord was the only true God. That's a win for Elijah, if you ask me. Nonetheless, in the very next chapter, Elijah plummeted into a depression. Queen Jezebel threatened his life, so Elijah ran away in fear. He even asked God to kill him. The day that began with Elijah's success ended with his fear.

I share this story because it reminds us that even the best Christians can face bouts of depression and doubt. Even those who hear from God on a regular basis can become so depressed they don't want to continue living.

As I was writing this book, the actor and comedian Robin Williams took his life. The news anchors, blog writers, and reporters all seemed to talk about a common lesson his death taught us: that suicide is no discriminator of persons. Depression can attack the rich as well as the poor. It can strike any race or ethnicity. It affects both believers and unbelievers. Struggling with depression does not make us any less of a Christian. Satan might try to convince us otherwise, but the truth is, doubt and depression are not sin. It's what we do with our doubts that matters.

One thing I love about God is that He doesn't back away from us when we're depressed. Depression might scare friends or family, but it doesn't scare God. He won't run the other way when we doubt Him. Instead, He comes to us in our defeat. In Elijah's case, He sent an angel and food to nourish him. In our cases, He might send a Bible verse at just the right time or a word of encouragement from a friend. He might send a prayer.

I don't know how He'll do it, but I do know this: God doesn't leave us alone when we need Him. He comes to us in our times of need and refreshes us with His presence. The same hand that nourished Elijah can — and will — nourish us as well.

QUESTIONS FOR REFLECTION

1. How has God encouraged you in times of sorrow?
2. How can God use other people to encourage His children?
3. Has God ever used you to encourage someone else?

PRAYER

Thank God for the reminder that even the strongest Christians struggle with doubts and depression. Ask God to remind you of His love for you and to nourish your spirit just as He nourished Elijah's.

SCRIPTURES FOR FURTHER MEDITATION

Hebrews 13:5, Romans 8:35–39

JOURNAL ACTIVITY

Write the second half of Hebrews 13:5 in your journal: "God has said, 'Never will I leave you; never will I forsake you.'" Work to memorize this verse throughout the remainder of the week.

TAKEAWAY

When you did nothing wrong, let God nourish your spirit.

ADDITIONAL NOTE

If you are struggling with suicidal thoughts, please get help *today*. Call 1-800-273-8255, the National Suicide Prevention Lifeline.

Peter in Prison

Scripture reading: Acts 12:1–6

"It was about this time that King Herod arrested some who belonged to the church, intending to persecute them. He had James, the brother of John, put to death with the sword. When he saw that this met with approval among the Jews, he proceeded to seize Peter also." — Acts 12:1–3

Ever since my son was born, I've had insomnia. It's improved over the years but is still a problem at times. People with insomnia often fall into two categories — those who can't fall asleep and those who wake throughout the night. I'm in the first category. Some nights, I lie in bed until two or three in the morning without ever getting to sleep. My body is tired, but my mind won't let it rest.

My husband, on the other hand, can sleep anytime, anywhere. Once, he fell asleep with a hard, plastic shape-sorter toy beneath his head as a pillow.

One of the reasons I can't sleep and my husband can is because I fail to let things go throughout the day. My husband forgives quickly and forgets easily. He knows he can't control everything about his life, so he doesn't attempt to. Me, not so much. If there's conflict before bed, I'm too upset to sleep. If I have a presentation to give the next day, I'm too nervous. If a child is sick, I'm too worried. To be completely honest, many of the times I can't sleep, it's because I haven't learned to relax in the arms of my loving Father.

The biography on the back of this book says I trust Him with my life, but sometimes my insomnia says otherwise.[2] In reality, I struggle to trust God. I fear He might not have everything under control. Worse, I fear His plans for my life might include some struggles I'd prefer to bypass.

Jeremiah 29:11 says, "'For I know the plans I have for you,' declares the LORD, 'plans to prosper you and not to harm you, plans to give you hope and a future.'" This is one of my favorite Bible verses, but did you realize when Jeremiah said this, he was also encouraging the Israelites to stay in captivity for many more years? In essence, Jeremiah told them, "God has plans for you, and they're great plans. Someday, God is going to bring you home. But that day isn't today. God's plans for you today are to stay where you are. Stay in captivity, away from everything you know and everyone you love." God had plans to prosper the Israelites, but only after a season of difficulty. There are days I fear God's plans are similar for my life. I know His plans are good, but I worry the good will follow the bad. Sometimes, I worry about the pain He might allow.

Because of my struggles with insomnia, Peter's actions in Acts 12 impress me. At the beginning of this chapter, King Herod arrested and persecuted several of the leaders of the early church. He even had James, one of Jesus' original disciples, put to death by the sword. Then Herod arrested Peter, put him in prison, and planned to bring him out for a public trial after the Passover ended.

On the night before Peter's trial, the text says, Peter was sleeping between two soldiers and bound with two chains. The conditions of the prison were certainly not ideal for sleeping. Have you ever tried to sleep with someone watching you? For me, it's impossible. Peter, though, had two men staring at him all night long and was still able to sleep. He also had chains wrapped around his body, making sleep even harder to find.

Add to these conditions the anticipation of the next day's events, and it's amazing Peter could rest at all. Herod had already killed James, and it's likely he planned to do the same to Peter. Peter knew this, so how was he able to rest, knowing death awaited him on the other side of the night?

It was because Peter knew who held his life in His hands. The Psalmist said, "Praise be to the Lord, to God our Savior, who daily bears our burdens." (Ps. 68:19) Peter could sleep because he allowed God to bear his burdens. Even though Peter hadn't done anything wrong to land himself in prison, he didn't fixate his thoughts on the unfairness of his situation. Instead, he fixated his thoughts on the One who promised to make all things right.

One other possible reason Peter was able to sleep is because he learned from the example of someone else months earlier. In Matthew 8, Jesus, Peter, and the other disciples were caught in a terrible storm. The disciples feared for their lives. Jesus, in contrast, slept peacefully in the boat. Maybe Peter was able to sleep in the prison because he had watched Jesus sleep in the storm. He finally got it. He understood that those who trust in the Lord could rest, even if storms rage around them.

QUESTIONS FOR REFLECTION

1. How is rest related to trust?
2. Have you ever experienced God's peace, even when a storm was raging around you? If so, please explain.

PRAYER

Ask God to give you rest. Pray He would help you find His peace, even when storms rage all around you.

SCRIPTURES FOR FURTHER MEDITATION

Psalm 68:19, Psalm 62:1–2, Hebrews 4:1–11,
Psalm 73:26, Matthew 11:28

JOURNAL ACTIVITY

Search for and listen to the song "Oceans" by Hillsong United. What lyrics in this song spoke to you today? Write them in your journal.

TAKEAWAY

When you did nothing wrong, rest in the knowledge
God has your life in His hands.

Jesus

Scripture reading: Luke 23:1–46

*"Father, forgive them, for they do not know
what they are doing." — Luke 23:34*

E arly one morning, Laurie Coombs received a phone call from her aunt, asking her to come over to her house as soon as possible. As Laurie's aunt opened her front door and locked eyes with Laurie, Laurie knew in that moment something was terribly wrong. The unthinkable had happened. Her father had been murdered.

"No, no, no, no" was all Laurie could get out. For years, as you can imagine, Laurie tried to work through her anger at her father's murderer, who was serving a sentence in prison for his crime. She even thought she had forgiven him… at least somewhat.

But nine and a half years later, Laurie felt God calling her to more than just forgiveness. She believed God wanted her to love her father's murderer — not just forgive him with her words but also love him with her actions. She began corresponding with Anthony on a regular basis and eventually led her father's killer to the Lord.

In one of Anthony's letters, he told Laurie, "Not only had you forgiven me, but you'd encouraged me."[3]

That kind of transformation only happens when someone chooses to follow in Jesus' footsteps. In Laurie's testimony video, she admitted forgiveness isn't easy. Neither is loving those who have hurt you. Regardless, this is exactly what Jesus asked us to do.

In the devotional for Day One this week, we talked about Esau and how he chose to forgive his brother. It's one thing to forgive someone for what he's done to you. That is hard enough. But today, we're going to take it one step further. We're going to take it past forgiveness to love. Just as

Laurie chose to love the man who killed her dad, we're going to look at the One who loved the people as they murdered Him.

Jesus didn't only forgive His enemies, He also prayed blessings upon their lives. He didn't pray for God to punish them, as would have been understandable, or for God to send them directly to hell for what they were doing to Him.

Instead, even as they beat Him, spat upon Him, made fun of Him, and ultimately killed Him, Jesus prayed for them. He prayed God would forgive them for what they were doing to Him. Even as He hung on the cross for sins He didn't commit, Jesus said, "Father, forgive them, for they do not know what they are doing." (Luke 23:34)

Peter described Jesus' actions in 1 Peter 2:23. "When they hurled their insults at him, he did not retaliate; when he suffered, he made no threats. Instead, he entrusted himself to him who judges justly." Jesus didn't seek revenge because, according to this verse, He entrusted Himself to the One True Judge, God the Father.

I love the word entrust. It means putting something into someone's care and trusting him or her to keep it safe. Jesus was able to love His enemies as they murdered Him because He trusted His Father with His life and with His death. He knew as long as God had Him, there was nothing His enemies could really do to Him.

Sure, they would whip Him. Sure, they could kill Him on an old wooden cross. But they could not keep Him in that grave. Not when God was in charge.

Max Lucado, in his book *Before Amen,* said, "You are never more like Jesus than when you pray for others."[4] This is especially true in regard to those who have hurt you. Praying for an enemy goes against everything we've been taught in America. We're taught to not let anyone take advantage of us and to stand up for ourselves. We're taught it's only the weak that allow themselves to be hurt without seeking revenge.

Jesus showed us another way. "You have heard that it was said, 'Love your neighbor and hate your enemy.' But I tell you, love your enemies and pray for those who persecute you." (Matthew 5:43–44)

Laurie has done this, even with the man who murdered her father.

Others in the Bible have done it too. Think of Joseph, who loved his brothers after they sold him into slavery. Think of Stephen, who, like Jesus, prayed for his murderers as they heaved stones at his head. These biblical figures, and others like them, were never more like Jesus than when they loved their enemies. Now, it's our turn to follow in His steps.

QUESTIONS FOR REFLECTION

1. Which do you think is harder: to forgive someone who has hurt you or to pray for God to bless this person? Why?
2. Sometimes, it feels almost impossible to pray for God to bless someone who has hurt us. How do you think people are able to do this?

PRAYER

Ask God to help you pray for those who have hurt you. Pray He would help you forgive, and ask Him to give you His eyes and to see your enemy as He sees him.

SCRIPTURES FOR FURTHER MEDITATION

1 Peter 2:19–23, Matthew 5:43–48, Luke 6:27

JOURNAL ACTIVITY

For whom do you need to pray today? Whom would you classify as your enemy? Write each person's name in your journal. Then, if you're willing, pray blessings over these names.

TAKEAWAY

When you did nothing wrong, pray for and love those who did.

When You Only Have Yourself to Blame

Sometimes, the most difficult person to forgive is yourself. Maybe you breezed through last week's devotionals. It's not hard for you to forgive other people. You assume the best in your friends and family and are quick to release hurt feelings.

But what about the hurts you've caused? Sometimes, even those who can forgive others struggle to forgive themselves. Maybe you've read all the Bible verses about how nothing can separate you from God's love and how Christ's sacrifice is a once and for all deal, but you still wonder how God could forgive you.

This week, we're going to look at five Bible stories in which the main characters had no one to blame for their pain but themselves. We'll look at the woman caught in adultery and study Jesus' response to her. We'll also study the lives of Jonah and David and look at the stories of the envious servants and the builders of the Tower of Babel. In each of these stories, the primary cause of suffering is the main characters themselves. These biblical figures couldn't blame anyone else for the pain they were enduring. Thankfully, even though they caused a large portion of their difficulties, God didn't leave any of them to suffer alone.

After you complete this week's lessons, please watch the video at...

www.crossrivermedia.com/portfolio/unbeaten-week-eight

The Woman Caught in Adultery

Scripture reading: John 8:1–11

"Jesus straightened up and asked her, 'Woman, where are they? Has no one condemned you?''No one, sir,' she said. 'Then neither do I condemn you,' Jesus declared. 'Go now and leave your life of sin.'" — *John 8:10–11*

She might have been wearing a blanket when they brought her to Jesus. *Might* have been. That's if the religious leaders gave her the chance to wrap the one she was lying on around her naked body before they dragged her out of the house. The text in John 8 says they caught her in the act of adultery. That means she probably had to leave her clothes and shoes where they had fallen. Her hair was probably tousled. What was meant to be an act done in secret was quickly becoming a public affair.

Who wouldn't notice a naked woman being dragged through the streets? Who wouldn't stop and stare as they made their way toward Jesus? And who wouldn't judge this woman for her sins?

Can you imagine how she must have felt? Humiliated to be sure. Probably also exposed, ashamed, and afraid.

She had good reason to feel all of these emotions. The Old Testament law commanded that anyone caught in adultery be stoned to death. This woman likely knew her fate. She knew what the religious leaders planned to do to her. She also knew she deserved it.

Have you ever done something that made you feel like you were no longer worthy of God's love? Maybe it felt good in the moment, but now the moment is gone and all you feel is shame.

Sometimes I wonder what this woman was thinking as the religious leaders plopped her down at the feet of Jesus. I wonder if she held her head down and refused to lift her eyes to look into Jesus'. She had heard about this man. Everyone said He was a good man. Some even said He was the Christ. She couldn't bear meet His eyes... not like this. Not wearing a blanket. Not wearing a hypothetical scarlet letter on her chest.

The longer He stood, the smaller she felt. She was a sinner. She was an adulterer. She was a word I can't even type here. She knew it, the religious leaders knew it, and Jesus knew it. Tears might have begun to fall from her eyes as she contemplated her actions. They were tears of shame and tears of embarrassment.

But then something happened. "Jesus bent down and started to write on the ground with his finger." (John 8:6) He might have even met her eyes as He was down there. She expected to see anger, judgment, and righteous indignation in those eyes. But instead, she saw love, a kind of love she had never seen before. She had never seen it in a man, not even in the man she had been with moments earlier. He had claimed to love her, of course, but when the religious leaders stormed in, he stormed out.

In the past, what she thought was love had been nothing but lust. There was something different about Jesus' eyes. When He looked at her, He didn't lust after her body as so many others did. He loved her, even when He knew her sins and even when she had nothing but brokenness to return to Him.

Finally, the religious leaders grew weary of waiting on Jesus. They demanded an answer from Him about what to do with the woman. "In the Law Moses commanded us to stone such women. Now what do you say?" (John 8:5)

Jesus told them the man who had no sin should be the first to throw a stone. With that, the religious leaders all slowly turned and walked away, one by one. Then Jesus said some of the most beautiful words in the entire biblical text. He asked the woman if all her accusers had left and then told her He would not condemn her either. "Go now and leave your life of sin." (John 8:11)

I don't know what you've done that you think is unforgiveable. I don't know the shame those sins have left on your heart. I do know Jesus doesn't want you to continue wearing that scarlet letter on your chest.

You might have been an adulterer in your past, but you don't have to be an adulterer in your future. You might have been a liar, an addict, a drunk, a prostitute, a cheater, a thief, or a murderer in your past, but you don't have to be any of these things in your future. Pride doesn't have to define who you are now. Neither does selfishness or vanity or worry or fear or whatever other sin has held you captive in the past.

When the woman caught in adultery was brought before Jesus, He didn't condemn her. He didn't belittle her for the mistakes she made. He didn't reject her. He didn't do any of the things we so often think Jesus will do to us after we sin.

What He did was love her and challenge her to sin no more. He asked her to make her future different than her past. Today, if you're clinging to the sins of your past because you fear God won't forgive you, give Him a chance. Jesus' sacrifice was plenty big enough to cover even the worst of sins.

QUESTIONS FOR REFLECTION

1. How do you imagine the woman felt as she was dragged through the streets after being caught in adultery?
2. This is a purely speculative question, so there are no right or wrong answers. Why do you think the religious leaders didn't drag the man before Jesus too?

PRAYER

Ask God to forgive you of your sins. Then ask Him to help you feel like you have been forgiven.

SCRIPTURES FOR FURTHER MEDITATION

Acts 3:19, Matthew 3:8, Luke 5:31–32, 1 John 1:9

JOURNAL ACTIVITY

On a blank page in your journal, write a list of sins you have committed recently. Then tear the sheet of paper from your journal and destroy it as a reminder that Jesus has already taken care of these sins. You don't need to hang on to them anymore.

TAKEAWAY

When you only have yourself to blame, go and sin no more.

Jonah

Scripture reading: Jonah 3:1–4:11

"When God saw what they did and how they turned from their evil ways, he relented and did not bring on them the destruction he had threatened. But to Jonah this seemed very wrong, and he became angry." — Jonah 3:10–4:1

I n 1987, David Berkowitz, a serial killer, made the news by claiming to be a new man, a born-again Christian. This transformation happened while Berkowitz was in prison for the atrocious crimes he committed. He made the news again in 2011 when he decided not to seek parole. His reason — he was already free in Jesus Christ.

A similar story occurred in 1994 when Jeffrey Dahmer, a convicted killer, sex offender, and cannibal, claimed he gave his life to Jesus.

These two men, if their claims are true, will probably be in heaven someday. First John 1:9 promises, "If we confess our sins, he is faithful and just and will forgive us our sins and purify us from all unrighteousness." We love this verse when it's referring to our own sins, but it is a more difficult truth to swallow when it's referring to murderers. One brave person even admitted his or her struggle over Dahmer's conversion, "If Jeffrey Dahmer is going to heaven, then I don't want to be there."[1]

It's hard to see people receive grace when they deserve punishment, isn't it? This is especially true when the sins they commit are what we would consider atrocious. We want to be forgiven when we sin, but we don't always want God to be as kind and compassionate to others.

That's the battle that raged within Jonah. When the people of Nineveh repented of their sins, God forgave them. He changed His mind about the punishment and instead offered grace.

Jonah wasn't happy about God's decision. He wanted the Ninevites punished, not forgiven. Taken captive, not freed from their bondage to sin. In fact, Jonah admitted that was why he ran away in the first place. (Jonah 4:2) When God told Jonah to go the city of Nineveh and preach about repentance, Jonah boarded a ship and ran away because he knew God was loving and compassionate. He knew God would forgive the people if they changed their behavior, and he didn't want that to happen. In his mind, these people deserved punishment.

What kind of person actually wants another to suffer? Who avoids sharing the gospel message because they don't want the person to receive forgiveness? On the surface, Jonah's actions seem petty, childish, and mean.

In reality, however, Jonah's struggle is not quite as uncommon as we'd like to believe. How many of us have been angry when someone didn't receive the punishment they deserved?

Not long ago, I was in a car wreck that someone else caused. She was looking for her phone when she should have been looking at the road. What's worse, even though the police officer admitted the wreck was her fault, he didn't give her a ticket. There were no legal consequences for her poor choices. Her insurance paid for both cars to be fixed, and she didn't get a ticket. I remember thinking, "How is she ever going to learn if there are no consequences?"

Why is it we are so quick to dole out punishment and judgment on others, but so slow to accept it ourselves? When we do something wrong, we want grace and mercy, but when someone else does something wrong, we want justice.

When my oldest child was about three or four, my husband and I created a Consequence Can out of an old can of formula. We wrote ten or so consequences on pieces of paper, folded them, and placed them in the can. Whenever my son did something wrong, he chose a consequence from the can. My favorite thing about the can was a little piece of paper that simply said *Grace*. When he chose this piece of paper, we showered him with mercy and grace instead of the consequence his behavior deserved. We wanted to teach him at an early age about God's grace and the grace we could give those around us.

One of the reasons I believe God included the book of Jonah in the Bible is to teach grown-ups about grace. We might not have a Consequence Can to learn from, but we do have God's question to Jonah at the end of the book. "Should I not have concern for the great city of Nineveh?" (Jonah 4:11)

The question isn't really about God. It's about us. We know God is concerned, but are we? Or do we get upset when someone else is on the receiving end of the love of God? Do we rejoice with those whom God has blessed, or do we pout and fuss because they don't deserve it or because we want a more generous helping for ourselves?

QUESTIONS FOR REFLECTION

1. When have you been frustrated by God's grace and mercy?
2. Why do you think Christians have a tendency to rate sins?

PRAYER

Ask God's forgiveness for times when you might have sought another person's punishment. Pray to become a person of grace, instead of a person always seeking justice.

SCRIPTURES FOR FURTHER MEDITATION

Romans 3:22–24, Ephesians 4:1–7, Ephesians 2:8–9

JOURNAL ACTIVITY

In your journal, jot down two lists: one list for the really bad sins and another for the not-so-bad ones. Write Romans 3:22–24 below your lists. How do these verses apply to this devotional?

TAKEAWAY

When you only have yourself to blame,
rejoice over God's grace instead of pouting about it.

David

Scripture reading: 2 Samuel 12:1–23

*"Then David said to Nathan, 'I have sinned
against the Lᴏʀᴅ." — 2 Samuel 12:13*

I had been a follower of Jesus for over fifteen years before I realized God's goal wasn't to make me happy.

Granted, I never actually said it aloud. I didn't admit I thought God wanted me to have a smile on my face. Still, that was how I acted. If anything didn't go my way, I cried for God to come to my rescue. Then, if He didn't, I questioned Him, as if He wanted nothing more than for little old me to be happy with life again.

This was especially the case with my miscarriages. I struggled to reconcile my belief that God wanted me to be happy with the reality of my unhappiness. I assumed since I followed Jesus my dreams and plans were from Him and He would make them come true. Psalm 37:4 was one of my favorite Bible verses. "Take delight in the Lᴏʀᴅ, and he will give you the desires of your heart." What I failed to realize was the key part of this verse was the beginning, not the end. I focused on the end of the verse, me getting the desires of my heart, when I should have focused on delighting in God.

What I finally learned was that Psalm 37:4 isn't a promise that God will give us everything we want. Instead, it's a challenge to align our hearts with His, to seek Him more than anything else, and to listen to the Holy Spirit and to the wisdom found in His Word. The truth is, when we find our delight in God, we don't need anything else.

Another verse that could easily mislead if the context is ignored is Luke 11:9, which says, "Ask and it will be given to you; seek and you will find; knock and the door will be opened to you." This verse, and others like it, seems to imply God will give us whatever we ask of Him. The truth is, this verse isn't meant to be a prescription for our happiness. Instead, it's meant to be a challenge to pray without ceasing. In fact, in context, it's not even referring to us asking for a child or a husband or a job or whatever. It's referring to us asking for the Holy Spirit. If we ask for the Holy Spirit, He will give it.

The key to studying verses like these is to look at contexts and to keep in mind the totality of Scripture. Don't base your beliefs on only one Bible verse, but on the totality of the Word. When I did this, I learned loving God doesn't guarantee an easy life. Just because we follow Jesus doesn't mean we'll always be happy, though it should mean we can always find joy. God's primary goal isn't our happiness. He is much more interested in our holiness than our happiness. God is much more interested in His name being known than in our lives being carefree.

This could not be more evident than in the life of David. In his lifetime, David faced one painful situation after another. Some of these difficulties weren't because of anything David did wrong. For example, when he ran for his life from King Saul, he hadn't done anything to cause Saul to chase him.

Other times, though, his difficulties were direct results of his sins. When David had an affair with Bathsheba and murdered her husband, Uriah, he faced serious consequences. David assumed since his actions were done in secret, no one knew. He forgot about God. God cared about David too much to allow him to face no consequences for his actions.

I have two little children. At times, it would be easier to look the other way about misbehavior. At the end of a long day, I don't always want to dish out consequences and deal with angry, tired boys. I have learned, though, not holding my children accountable is *not* what's best for them. They need consequences for poor choices so they become better people. I give them consequences, not because I *don't* love them, but because I *do*.

God does the same thing with us. He disciplines us because He loves us. Hebrews 12:7 says, "Endure hardship as discipline; God is treating you as his children." If God never gave us consequences, we would never learn to make better choices. If God never punished David for his sin with Bathsheba, what would have prevented him

144

from repeating his behavior?

God gave David a consequence because God loved David too much to look the other way. He loves us too much to look the other way too.

One thing I love about this text is David's response to God's discipline. He didn't get angry with God or curse Him for what He had done. He didn't pridefully refuse to take responsibility for his sins. Instead, he admitted his wrongs, prayed, and then worshipped God, even though God hadn't healed David's son.

I think the reason David was able to do this was because he recognized God's goal for David's life. God didn't only want David to be happy; He also wanted David to be holy. Holiness, both for David back then and for us today, can never happen without God's loving discipline.

QUESTIONS FOR REFLECTION

1. Have you ever believed God wants you to be happy? Why do you think so many Christians believe this? Do you think believers in other cultures struggle with this too?
2. What's the difference between joy and happiness? Why is it important to recognize the difference?
3. Why is accepting the Lord's discipline so difficult?

PRAYER

Pray for the ability to accept the Lord's discipline as David did.

SCRIPTURES FOR FURTHER MEDITATION

Hebrews 12:7–13, Proverbs 12:1,
Proverbs 3:11–12, Revelation 3:19

JOURNAL ACTIVITY

Write Hebrews 12:5–6 in your journal: "My son, do not make light of the Lord's discipline, and do not lose heart when he rebukes you, because the Lord disciplines the one he loves, and he chastens everyone he accepts as his son." Then read through Hebrews 12 down to verse 11. Make two columns in your journal: one titled "Human Fathers," the other titled "Heavenly Father." Using Hebrews 12:5–11, compare and contrast the discipline of each of these types of fathers in the two columns.

TAKEAWAY

When you only have yourself to blame,
accept the Lord's discipline as an act of love.

Hardworking (Envious) Servants

Scripture reading: Matthew 20:1–15

*"Are you envious because
I am generous?" — Matthew 20:15*

This might be the hardest devotional for me to write. I wish I didn't struggle with this and couldn't relate at all to this story. It's embarrassing to admit I'm envious of God's generosity to other people. What kind of person isn't happy when God answers the prayers of another? Apparently, it's the kind of person who has been let down in the past. It's the kind of person who has prayed for something over and over again and hasn't yet received the answer they long to hear. In the past two years, since the loss of our fourth baby, this struggle has been the primary way Satan attacks my heart.

So even though I'd like to bypass the theme of today's story, I can't in good conscious ignore it because I know I'm not the only one. There are others out there, maybe even some of you reading this, who struggle with envy and who long for something someone else has.

Six months ago, I received a text message from a friend. It was a group message with an ultrasound picture attached. "We have prayed, and the Lord has answered our prayer" was the message. Immediately, my mind jumped to my own situation. Why hasn't the Lord answered our prayer?

The next night, not even twenty-four hours later, I got another group text from another friend. "If you haven't heard, we're expecting!" Once again, my mind didn't rejoice with her, at least not at first. Instead, my heart sank. Again. God gave a baby to yet another friend, and my womb was still empty.

After that second message came through, a friend of mine sent me a text, "I'm praying for you. I know this is hard." She had been included in the group message, knew my struggle, and recognized how much the announcement must have hurt. She also challenged me. "You have to remember it's not about you. This is about her. This is about celebrating with her."

Ouch. One of the first articles I ever had published was about Romans 12:15. "Rejoice with those who rejoice; mourn with those who mourn." Nevertheless, here I was, refusing to rejoice with a friend because I was too focused on what I didn't have to rejoice with her on what she had been given.

Like the hardworking servants in Matthew 20, I was envious of God's generosity to someone else. Instead of remembering what He had already given to me, I focused on what He gave to another. My pain was self-induced. I chose envy; therefore, I chose pain.

Here's how the parable in Matthew 20 began. A landowner went into the marketplace early in the morning to hire workers for his vineyard. Later that day, at around nine in the morning, he returned to the marketplace and hired more workers. At noon, 3:00, and 5:00, he did the same, each time promising to pay his workers a fair wage.

At the end of the day, the owner of the vineyard asked his foreman to pay the workers, beginning with the last ones hired. He paid all the workers the same amount, even though some had worked all day and others only an hour. The men who were hired first were outraged. "These who were hired last worked only one hour,' they said, 'and you have made them equal to us who have borne the burden of the work and the heat of the day.'" (Matthew 20:12)

The owner reminded them they agreed to work for the amount he paid them. They had no right to be upset. Then he asked them a pointed question. "Don't I have the right to do what I want with my own money? Or are you envious because I am generous?" (Matthew 20:15)

In a similar way, doesn't God have the right to give whatever He wants to whomever He wants? Who am I to be angry when He gives to others or to judge His gifts to one person as better than another? I am not entitled to anything. I don't deserve anything from God. As hard as that is to write, it's true. God doesn't owe me a child, and He doesn't owe you anything either.

There's one huge problem with envy. It blinds us to our own blessings. It takes our eyes off what God has given us and fixes them on what He's given others. When we fixate on what others have, we bring pain upon ourselves.

There is a cure for envy, though — gratitude.

QUESTIONS FOR REFLECTION

1. When have you struggled with being envious of God's blessings on another?
2. How can gratitude destroy envy?

PRAYER

Ask God's forgiveness for when you have envied His generosity to others. Pray He would help you rejoice with those who rejoice, even while you wait for Him to answer your prayers.

SCRIPTURES FOR FURTHER MEDITATION

Romans 12:15, Philippians 2:3, 1 Corinthians 13:4–7, James 3:14–16, 1 Thessalonians 5:18

JOURNAL ACTIVITY

Earlier, I asked you to create a gratitude journal. Are you still writing in it? If not, get started again. Consider creating a journal for your family too. Leave it on the kitchen counter to write in each night at dinnertime. Ask each of your children to share three things for which they are thankful.

TAKEAWAY

When you only have yourself to blame, practice gratitude.

Builders of the Tower of Babel

Scripture reading: Genesis 11:1–9

"Then they said, 'Come, let us build ourselves a city, with a tower that reaches to the heavens, so that we may make a name for ourselves.'" — Genesis 11:4

My five-year-old son had pajama day at school yesterday. The only problem, he refused to wear pajamas. When I asked him why he didn't want to wear them, he looked down at the floor and told me a little girl would make fun of him and call him names if he wore his pj's. I reminded him his entire class would wear them, but this didn't change his mind. He still refused because someone might call him a name.

Names matter, don't they? I still remember the nickname people gave me in elementary school. They called me "Shorty" because of my height. It wasn't a terrible name and certainly could have been worse, but it nonetheless made me feel insecure about my size.

Another name was even more damaging to my heart as a pre-teen. My family and I went on a trip to Colorado one summer. While waiting in line to get on a ride of some sort, an older gentleman said to my two brothers and me, "You three boys go ahead." I stood there unmoved because I assumed he was talking to my brothers and my dad. Then he repeated himself, and I got it. He meant me. He thought I was a boy. Granted, I had my hair in a ponytail underneath a hat, and I was wearing athletic shorts and a T-shirt. I had yet to develop anything that made my physical body look feminine. Looking back, I don't blame the guy for thinking I looked like a boy. I probably did. Nonetheless, the damage was done.

For twenty years, I refused to wear hats because I thought they made me look like a boy. It was only this year, as a thirty-year-old woman, I finally felt comfortable enough in my womanhood to purchase a hat. A name someone I didn't even know gave me twenty years ago has dictated a portion of my life for years. Names stick, don't they, for better or for worse?

I think that's why in Genesis 11, the people wanted to make a good name for themselves. They, like us, wanted to be known for something great. They wanted people to look at them and think about the positive things they had done, rather than the negative. They knew names stuck and wanted theirs to be great.

One thing that's interesting about this text is the people caused the very thing they were trying to prevent. They built the tower to prevent themselves from being scattered, but that's exactly what happened. God confused their language and scattered them across the earth.

You and I can learn two lessons from this story. First of all, it's not wise to fight against God's plans. If God doesn't want a tower to be built, He's going to stop it from being constructed. If God doesn't want you to do something, He has ways of preventing it from happening. Instead of fighting against Him, bucking the system and trying to force your own way, choose instead to lean into His plans. They might not be yours, but they are better.

The second thing we can learn is, seeking to make a name for yourself is probably not going to turn out well. The people who built the Tower of Babel did become famous. Their story even made it into the most popular book of all time — the Bible. But that's not the kind of fame I want, and my guess is, it's not the kind you want either.

Also, did you notice that not one of the builders was listed by name? In other portions of Scripture, the writers listed hundreds of names. In fact, one of the lists is in the remaining verses of this chapter. But in this text, not one builder is listed by name. I wonder if maybe that's because even though they became famous as a group, they failed to make a name for themselves that mattered. They went down in history as the people who allowed pride to destroy them.

In our "get famous quick" culture with YouTube, Facebook, Twitter, and various other social media networks, it's easy to get sucked into the game of making a name for yourself. It's easy to live for applause. The truth is, the only names that will last are the ones we get from Jesus, and the only applause that matters is His.

The truth is, making a name for ourselves is unnecessary. Jesus has already given us a name that is far better than any name we could ever acquire ourselves. That name, my friends, is Child of God.

QUESTIONS FOR REFLECTION

1. What was so bad about the people building a tower to heaven?
2. Why do you think making a name for yourself is such a temptation in the culture we live in today?

PRAYER

Pray for an appropriate perspective: that God would help you think about making a name for Him, rather than a name for yourself.

SCRIPTURES FOR FURTHER MEDITATION

1 John 3:1, Proverbs 22:1

JOURNAL ACTIVITY

Search for the song "He Knows My Name" by Francesca Battistelli. As you listen, write in your journal any of the lyrics that spoke to your heart today.

TAKEAWAY

When you only have yourself to blame, forget any
painful nicknames and cling to the name Jesus gave you.

When the Future Isn't Clear

f I unbuckle my two-year-old son from his car seat and don't insist he get out of the car immediately, he inevitably climbs into the front. He puts both hands on the wheel and begins vrooming as fast as his little imagination will take him. If I have my purse or sunglasses or the diaper bag in that seat, he doesn't care. He shoves them out of his way, because he wants to drive!

Unfortunately, I'm often the same way in my relationship with God. I claim I want Him to control my life but then shove Him out of the way in a desperate attempt to get behind the wheel. This is especially true when the future isn't clear to me or when it's scary.

This week, we're going to look at five stories from the Bible of people who learned to trust God with unknown futures. Some of them, like the Israelites in the wilderness, struggled to give up the driver's seat. Others, like Abram and Sarai, the Proverbs 31 woman, and Mary the mother of Jesus, seemed to do it with very little fight. This week, we'll learn lessons from both.

After you complete this week's lessons, please watch the video at...

www.crossrivermedia.com/portfolio/unbeaten-week-nine

Abram and Sarai

Scripture reading: Genesis 12:1–4

*"The L*ORD* had said to Abram, 'Go from your country, your people and your father's household to the land I will show you.'"* — *Genesis 12:1*

A few years after my husband and I were married, I came home from work to find him sitting in the driveway with a packed car. He had arranged a surprise weekend trip for the two of us. I already admitted in the introduction to this week's study I struggle with giving control to God, and God is perfect! Imagine how hard it was for me to refrain from making sure my husband remembered to pack my hair dryer, makeup, toothbrush, and undergarments!

He took care of everything, even making sure our dog was fed while we were away. He packed for both of us, made reservations at a hotel, and planned the entire weekend. He even called my boss and arranged for me to miss work the next day. There was no reason for me to be nervous. Even so, pulling out of the driveway without checking my suitcase was one of the hardest things I have ever done. My husband laughs at me when we travel because I pack things just in case. There was no just in case luxuries for this trip. Instead, I had to live, at least for the two-hour drive, with the unknowns.

That trip was amazing and my husband had remembered everything I needed. Still, I prefer the known to the unknown. I like to be in control of my future. I like to know what's going on. My husband and I sit down each Sunday evening and discuss the week ahead. Both of us are planners. We don't like to be caught off guard with some unknown event.

What about you? Do you ever struggle with the unknowns of your life? Has God ever asked you to do something or go somewhere without making all the details clear?

Sometimes I wonder if Sarai and Abram had a disagreement when Abram told her God wanted them to pack their belongings and move. It doesn't appear they did from the specifics in the Scripture. That is amazing to me. I certainly wouldn't have been as easy-going if my husband told me God said we needed to move without giving any specifics as to where or when. I would have asked for more information.

As far as we know, though, neither Abram nor Sarai asked God for any specifics. "The LORD had said to Abram, 'Go from your country, your people and your father's household to the land I *will* show you.'" (Genesis 12:1, emphasis mine) Then, amazingly, it says, "Abram went." (Genesis 12:4) Just like that, he packed his belongings and headed to an unknown destination.

The more I have thought about this act of faith, the more impressed I have become with Abram and Sarai. It would have been amazing if they had done this after God did the miracle of giving them Isaac in their old age. But this happened before God showed Himself faithful with Isaac. They trusted God with their unknown future *before* God showed them He was trustworthy!

Abram and Sarai didn't know where they were headed, but they followed because they knew who was leading them.

Hebrews 11:1 says, "Now faith is confidence in what we hope for and assurance about what we do not see." Abram and Sarai didn't see their final destination or quite possibly even the road leading to the destination, but they followed because they knew Who led the way, and they had faith He who led them was faithful.

Later on, in that same chapter of Hebrews, the author says, "By faith Abraham, when called to go to a place he would later receive as his inheritance, obeyed and went, even though he did not know where he was going." (Hebrews 11:8)

You and I might not always know where God is leading us either. At times it might seem like He's not leading us anywhere or like He's not even there anymore. Those are the times we get the opportunity to trust like Abram and Sarai did. Those are the times we get the chance to trust our unknowns with the God who knows all.

QUESTIONS FOR REFLECTION

1. When have you struggled to trust God with the unknowns in your life?
2. What helps you trust God when your future isn't clear?

PRAYER

Ask God to help you trust Him with your future and with the unknowns in your life.

SCRIPTURES FOR FURTHER MEDITATION

Hebrews 11:8–16, Proverbs 3:5, Matthew 6:34

JOURNAL ACTIVITY

In an earlier devotional, I shared a quote by Corrie ten Boom: "Never be afraid to trust an unknown future to a known God." Write this quote in your journal. Then below it, write a prayer to God about your future. Share your fears and dreams, and then ask Him to help you trust.

TAKEAWAY

When the future isn't clear,
trust your unknowns to the God who knows all.

The Israelites in the Wilderness

Scripture reading: Exodus 13:17–18

"When Pharaoh let the people go, God did not lead them on the road through the Philistine country, though that was shorter. For God said, 'If they face war, they might change their minds and return to Egypt.' So God led the people around by the desert road toward the Red Sea." — Exodus 13:17–18

Yesterday I flipped the page of my calendar to October. Even though I love fall and the changing seasons, I'm not a fan of this particular month. In fact, October is the hardest month of the year for me. At times, I wish I could bypass it altogether: fall asleep on September 30 and then awaken on Halloween.

On October 15, four years ago, our first baby left the safety of my womb and went to her forever home in heaven. Each year since then, my husband and I light candles in memory of each of the children we have lost. (October 15 is also Pregnancy and Infant Loss Awareness Day, so October is a hard month for many babyloss survivors). Ever since that day four years ago, my husband and I have prayed for a healthy pregnancy, waited for God's answer, and heard nothing but silence.

That means we've been praying for about forty-eight months, 1,460 days. Though these past four years of unanswered prayers have felt like an eternity, it's nothing compared to the amount of time the Israelites had to wait for God to deliver them from Egypt. As I mentioned in an earlier devotional, they had to wait more than 400 years.

Then, when God finally answered their cries and delivered them from slavery, He did something no one expected. He led them into the desert instead of toward the Promised Land.

If you look at a map of ancient Egypt and Canaan, you can easily see the quickest route from Egypt to the Promised Land. It's almost straight east. We teach children at young ages that the shortest distance between two points is a straight line. Why, then, didn't God lead the Israelites on the straightest, shortest route to the Promised Land?

Why did He lead them south when they needed to go east? If God wanted them to reach a certain destination, why didn't He lead them there to begin with?

The answer can be found in Exodus 13. God led them on the detour because He knew they would face war on the shorter route, get scared, and turn back to Egypt. As it turns out, God had good reason for leading them in what appeared like circles in the desert. He knew He was dealing with fickle people, and He knew they needed that time in the desert to mature.

Sometimes, I think God might do the same thing with us. He knows things we don't, so He leads us in ways we might not understand. A friend of mine miscarried a baby years ago and couldn't understand why God allowed the loss. Then, at right about the time that baby would have been due, she discovered her husband was having an affair. I don't believe God caused the miscarriage, but I do think it's possible He allowed it because He knew what lay on the road in front of my friend.

Think of it this way. It's like God is an airplane pilot, hovering above the road we are driving on. Because of His vantage point, He can see things we can't see. Imagine if He saw a terrible car wreck about a mile ahead of us. He calls and tells us to take the next exit. We might question Him because we don't see the traffic or the wreck. We might question Him because we think we know the best way to get to our destination. Nonetheless, His directions would be the best way to go.

Because He can see things we can't, He sometimes leads us in ways that don't make sense. Another thing to consider is that sometimes, God is more interested in the people we become than in the places we go. He's more interested in the road we take to get somewhere than in the destination itself. What I mean is this: there are some character traits that can only be developed under pressure.

Romans 5:3–4 says it this way: "We also glory in our sufferings, because we know that suffering produces perseverance; perseverance, character; and character, hope." God might be willing to take us on a detour because He knows the detour will help us become better people. He knows we need the detour to strengthen us for the road ahead and to build within us perseverance, character, and hope.

So here's the question of the day: what do you do when God doesn't seem to be leading you anywhere, when it feels like He's taking you in circles through a desert?

You do what the Israelites did. You continue to follow the pillar of cloud by day and the pillar of fire by night. You go where He tells you to go, even if it doesn't make sense. And you trust the pilot because He might see something you can't see.

QUESTIONS FOR REFLECTION

1. When has your life taken an unexpected detour?
2. How might God want to use this detour to develop your character?

PRAYER

Pray for God to enable you to follow Him, even when He seems to be leading you off the path.

SCRIPTURES FOR FURTHER MEDITATION

Isaiah 55:8–9, Psalm 147:5

JOURNAL ACTIVITY

Draw a road in your journal with a detour sign beside the road. Then write below the detour sign: "Sometimes we need the detours."

TAKEAWAY

When the future isn't clear, follow the One who can see things you can't.

The Proverbs 31 Woman

Scripture reading: Proverbs 31:10–31

*"She is clothed with strength and dignity; she
can laugh at the days to come." — Proverbs 31:25*

Two days ago, a friend of mine buried her five-month-old baby
girl. This sweet, beautiful child died unexpectedly. One day she
was completely healthy, at least as far as her parents could tell.
The next she seemed to have a slight cold. Then, less than twenty-four
hours later, she passed from this earth into the next. She left behind
two broken-hearted parents and siblings who are now trying to figure
out this whole "death thing" way too soon.

How do you move forward after something like that happens? How
do you ever get to a place in which you don't fear for your other children? If it happened to one child, what's stopping it from happening to
another? If God allowed it once, who is to say He won't allow it again?

God doesn't want us to live in fear of the future, but it's hard not to. As
I write, ISIS is threatening Christian families across the world. Terrorists
are killing not only grown men and women but also children and babies.
The first confirmed cases of a dangerous virus called Ebola have also
reached the United States. Another virus called Enterovirus is attacking
the country, often striking young children. Last night on the news, I listened to a report of a preschool boy who showed no signs or symptoms
when he went to bed in the evening but didn't wake in the morning.

How can we not live in fear with these terrifying problems going on
around us? The Proverbs 31 woman was able to laugh at the days to come.
This is a woman who wasn't fearful of the future as many of us are. Even
though she's probably not a real person but rather an ideal person whom
we can try to emulate, I nonetheless have this picture of her in my mind.

I picture her with her head thrown back, laughing at the top of her lungs. Just as a child can't stop giggling when he's being tickled, I picture her unable to control her laughter. Though she could easily fear the unknowns of the future, she chooses instead to laugh at the days to come. Her face radiates joy, even when her future might be scary.

I think the reason she is able to do this is recorded in verse 30: "A woman who fears the LORD is to be praised." The Proverbs 31 woman feared God, and that holy fear of the Lord enabled her to face her future without fear. She knew her life was in God's hands and trusted that whatever He allowed into her life, He would also strengthen her for.

As I've thought about this text, I've realized something that has drastically altered my thinking. Fear of God and fear of the future are mutually exclusive. You can't fear God and at the same time fear the future. If you truly fear God in a biblical way, acknowledging Him as the One who controls your days, you don't have any reason to fear anything else.

Psalm 27:1 says it this way, "The LORD is my light and my salvation — whom shall I fear? The LORD is the stronghold of my life — of whom shall I be afraid?" The reason we don't need to fear is because God is good and controls our futures, so we know He won't allow anything into our lives He won't also help us endure.

This unfortunately doesn't mean He won't allow difficult things. He might allow pain. He might allow death. But know this — death was never part of God's original design for us. We were not made for death, we were made for life. That's why death hurts so much. First Thessalonians 4 encourages believers to grieve differently than the rest of the world. Why? Because we still have hope. Yes, death hurts. It's unnatural. It's heartbreaking. But it's not the end, so we grieve differently.

At the graveside service of my friend's baby, as I watched a too-small casket being lowered into the ground, I remembered Psalm 46:1–3, which says, "God is our refuge and strength, an ever-present help in trouble. Therefore we will not fear, though the earth give way and the mountains fall into the heart of the sea, though its waters roar and foam and the mountains quake with their surging."

My friends aren't naïve to the pain of this world, especially not now. But they don't grieve as those who have no hope. They grieve as those who know their ever-present help in times of trouble. They are trusting God with their lives, even when their circumstances suggest He's not trustworthy. They fear Him, instead of fearing the future. Because of that, I know they will find laughter again. As Psalm 30:5 promises, "weeping may stay for the night, but rejoicing comes in the morning."

QUESTIONS FOR REFLECTION

1. What do you most fear about the future?
2. What's the difference between fearing God and fearing the future? Do you agree or disagree that you can't fear both at the same time?

PRAYER

Ask God to help you learn to fear and revere Him instead of fearing the future. Pray for Him to help you entrust your fears into His capable hands.

SCRIPTURES FOR FURTHER MEDITATION

Psalm 27:1, Psalm 118:6, Psalm 56:3-4,
Romans 8:15, 1 John 4:18, Matthew 10:28

JOURNAL ACTIVITY

Read Proverbs 31:10-31. As you read, make a list in your journal of some of the characteristics of the Proverbs 31 woman. For instance, in verse 20, you could write that she is generous. Do you think any of these qualities helped her not fear for the future?

TAKEAWAY

When the future isn't clear, don't fear the days to come.
Fear the One who holds your days.

Mary, Jesus' Mother

Scripture reading: Luke 1:26–38

> *"'I am the Lord's servant,' Mary answered.
> 'May your word to me be fulfilled.'" — Luke 1:38*

A few weeks ago, I chatted with my friend Erin. For the previous two months, she has tried to teach her baby how to go to sleep on his own. Her son, Dominic, isn't interested. He'd much rather be rocked to sleep in the arms of his loving mama than learn to fall asleep by himself. As she described their interaction to me, she told me, "I kept telling him, 'You need to rest. I know you don't realize you need sleep, but you need to trust me. Trust I know what's best for you.'"

Sometimes I think God is like that with us too. He's watching us fight against what He's trying to do in our lives and longs to hold us in His arms, caress our tear-stained faces, and ask us to trust Him. We're flailing around like a newborn baby fighting sleep when what we really need to do is trust in the One who's holding us in His arms.

Even more than a parent knows what's best for a child, our God knows what's best for us. That doesn't mean it's easy to trust Him, though.

When life doesn't turn out as planned and we're not sure what the future holds, it's hard to trust God when it feels like He's turning our well-laid plans upside down.

One biblical figure who probably understood more than most what it's like to have God change her plans was Mary, the mother of Jesus. When God chose her to be the mother of His Son, He sent an angel to tell her the "good" news. I put "good" in quotes because even though it was good news, to her and to us, it probably didn't feel like good news at the time.

Mary was a young virgin, engaged to the man of her dreams, when the angel visited her. Think about how the angel's announcement would have threatened Mary's plans. Her engagement was in trouble, because Joseph, a God-fearing, righteous man, wouldn't want to marry a woman who wasn't a virgin. Her reputation was in trouble because no one would believe she had not been impure. Her livelihood was in trouble, because if Joseph refused to marry her and the entire town viewed her as an immoral woman, she would have difficulty ever finding someone to provide for her. God's good news shattered Mary's plans for her life.

Even still, Mary agreed to God's plan. "'I am the Lord's servant,' Mary answered. 'May your word to me be fulfilled.'" (Luke 1:38) God wrecked Mary's plans, but she submitted, because she knew God was trustworthy. He turned her life upside down, but she recognized upside down to her was exactly as God intended.

Maybe God changed your plans too. Maybe the life you thought you'd have isn't turning out like you imagined. Most people, when they dream of their futures, don't picture cancer in their lives. Most don't picture divorce, bankruptcy, sickness, widowhood, or the death of a loved one too soon.

Because most of us grow up watching movies like *Cinderella* and *Beauty and the Beast,* we expect our lives to have the happily ever after too. We don't expect our Prince Charming to cheat on us or break our hearts. We can't fathom the day our life unravels.

We want the fairy tale ending, but we forget that even in fairy tales, the hero must fight the villain before the happily ever after. My question to us today is, are we willing to give up our fairy tale endings? Are we willing — if God asks — to let go of our plans for our lives and grab hold of His?

Mary's life wasn't easy after she accepted God's plan for her life. She even watched her thirty-three-year-old son die on a wooden cross. Her life wasn't comfortable, but it was blessed. Matthew 5:4 says this, "Blessed are those who mourn, for they will be comforted."

God's plan for you might not be easy either. It might include difficulty, pain, and seasons of uncertainty. But it too will be blessed, just as Mary's was. You, too, will be comforted by the Hand that holds you.

There's something absolutely amazing about a baby sleeping in his parent's arms. It's a picture of trust. The world might be crazy around him, but he's okay when he's in his parent's arms. Friends, your world might be crazy too. It might be the exact opposite of what you dreamed it would be. Nonetheless, if you are trusting in the arms that are holding you, you are exactly where you need to be and you are going to be okay.

QUESTIONS FOR REFLECTION

1. In what ways has God changed your plans for your life?
2. What one thing do you think would be hardest for you to give up if God asked? Why?

PRAYER

Pray for God to help you be like Mary and submit to His plan for your life, even if it is different than your own.

SCRIPTURES FOR FURTHER MEDITATION

Jeremiah 29:11, Proverbs 16:9

JOURNAL ACTIVITY

Write Matthew 5:4 in your journal: "Blessed are those who mourn, for they will be comforted." How do you think those who mourn are blessed? This week, work to memorize this verse.

TAKEAWAY

When the future isn't clear, give up the fairy tale
and submit to God's plan for your life.

John

Scripture reading: Revelation 1:1–19

*"When I saw him, I fell at his feet as though dead.
Then he placed his right hand on me and said:
'Do not be afraid. I am the First and the Last.
I am the Living One; I was dead, and now look,
I am alive for ever and ever! And I hold the keys
of death and Hades.'" — Revelation 1:17–18*

I recently watched the movie *Rise of the Guardians* with my children. There's a scene at the end of the movie where a child is afraid he'll stop believing in the guardians. If you're not familiar with the movie, the guardians are Santa Clause, the Easter Bunny, Jack Frost, the Sandman, and the Tooth Fairy. The premise behind the movie is that the guardians only have power when the children believe in them. If the kids stop believing, the guardians lose their power and are unable to protect the children from the Boogey Man.

In one of the closing scenes, the child looked at Jack Frost with worry in his eyes, "What if we stop believing again?"

Jack looked intently at the boy. "Hey, hey, slow down, slow down. You telling me you stop believing in the moon when the sun comes out?… Do you stop believing in the sun when clouds block it out?"

The boy relaxed as Jack's comment appeared to sink in. "No."

The reason I love this scene so much is because it's a reminder to us we don't have to see God to believe in Him. When the clouds block the sun, we don't stop believing in the sun's existence. When the moon disappears for the day, we don't stop believing it's there. We know it exists even when we can't see it.

It's the same way with God. We don't have to see Him all the time to know He's with us. What's amazing is that sometimes He gives us a glimpse anyway. Sometimes, maybe for our good and maybe for the good of someone else, God lets us take a peek at His glory.

He did it for Moses in Exodus 33, for Isaiah in Isaiah 6, and for Jacob in Genesis 32. In the New Testament, He did it for Stephen in Acts 7 and for Paul on the road to Damascus in Acts 9. Those who saw Jesus when He walked on this earth also got a peek at God. The biblical figure I want to focus on today is the disciple John.

He caught a glimpse of God when he followed Jesus around Israel. But later on, he got an even more amazing vision of the Almighty God.

Most of Jesus' original disciples were killed for their faith. John was the exception. Instead of becoming a martyr, he was exiled to the island of Patmos. While in exile, Jesus showed himself to John. As you can imagine, John was frightened. In Revelation 1:17–18, he said, "When I saw him, I fell at his feet as though dead. Then he placed his right hand on me and said: 'Do not be afraid. I am the First and the Last. I am the Living One; I was dead, and now look, I am alive for ever and ever! And I hold the keys of death and Hades.'"

Since we exist on this side of heaven, we don't have the opportunity to ask God why He appeared to some people and not to others. We don't yet get to discover why John was chosen to receive the vision of heaven.

I wonder, though, if it might have been because John was struggling. Maybe God chose John to take a peek into heaven because John needed to see what his future held. Or, on the other hand, maybe God chose John because God knew his disciple would be faithful to share the vision with others.

God knew there would be days when we would doubt. Days when, like the child in *Rise of the Guardians*, we would worry about the future and worry we might stop believing. Maybe God chose John because He knew John would share the vision with the early church and with us today.

Whatever the reason, one thing we do know is this: John's vision back then makes all the difference today. What John saw on that island of Patmos years ago changes our lives now.

He saw Jesus riding on a glorious horse, victorious over the devil, death, and all things that Satan meant to destroy us by. He saw heaven, the magnificent place Jesus has prepared for each of us who have chosen to trust in Him. He saw the saints, worshipping before God in beautiful song. And he saw God, the one who would wipe away every tear from our eyes.

John didn't know what his future held. From the looks of it, he might die on an island, alone and forgotten by most. He didn't know his future, but because of the glimpse God provided John knew he had no reason to fear. Whatever lay ahead of him, whether torture, years of exile, or death, these things were nothing compared to the inheritance God had prepared for him in heaven.

QUESTIONS FOR REFLECTION

1. How does heaven affect your perspective?
2. The Bible tells us to fix our eyes heavenward, but it is often easier said than done. What helps you focus on heaven?

PRAYER

Ask God to encourage your spirit with the reality of heaven. Pray He would help you fix your gaze on heaven instead of the things of today.

SCRIPTURES FOR FURTHER MEDITATION

Psalm 121:1–2, Psalm 123:1, Philippians 3:14

JOURNAL ACTIVITY

In *Rise of the Guardians,* the guardians lost their power when the kids stopped believing in them. In your journal answer this: If God worked that way (He doesn't), how much power do you think He would have?

TAKEAWAY

When the future isn't clear, fix your gaze on eternity.

When You Are Searching for Answers

My husband and I took our boys to a new ice cream shop last weekend. It was a novelty ice cream store that froze the ice cream right in front of us using liquid nitrogen. We don't normally drive long distances for ice cream, but couldn't resist trying this new store, which was about thirty minutes from our home.

On the way, my five-year-old asked question after question. I don't remember what topic he was interested in, but I do remember thinking, "Wow, he has a lot of questions!"

Asking questions is an inevitable part of childhood. It's also an inevitable part of being a believer. At some point or another, most of us are going to have some questions for God, questions like "why me?" or "how is this possible?" or "whose fault is this?" or others.

Throughout this final week of study, as we look at the lives of Job, Peter, Judas, the man who was born blind, and the early disciples, we're going to discuss some of the questions many of us ask when life gets hard. On the final day of this week, we'll look at the One who holds the answers.

After you complete this week's lessons, please watch the video at...
www.crossrivermedia.com/portfolio/unbeaten-week-ten

Job

Scripture reading: Job 42:1-17

*"Surely I spoke of things I did not understand,
things too wonderful for me to know." — Job 42:3*

My five-year-old son has selective hearing. When I ask him a question, he doesn't always answer me, especially when he's in the middle of doing something else. This morning, as I tried to get him ready for school, I asked him what he wanted for breakfast — toast or cereal.

Two options. It shouldn't be that difficult. At least that's what I thought. What I failed to realize was he was too busy watching his pet fish to answer.

"Toast or cereal?" I repeated twice, still with no answer.

By this time, I was frustrated. When I ask a question, I expect an answer. Silence doesn't work well for me. Can you relate? When you ask a question, you expect an answer. Of course, the answer might not be what you'd like, but you expect an answer anyway. At least I do.

In Job's case, though, God didn't offer answers. Job pelted Him with questions about why He allowed the tragedies of Job's life, but God didn't answer a single one. Instead, He turned the whole conversation around and asked Job, "Where were you when I laid the earth's foundation? Tell me, if you understand." (Job 38:4)

For nearly four chapters in the book of Job, God challenged him to think about his position in life. In essence, He said to Job: "Since you clearly know so much about how the world works, why don't you tell me about its inner workings: how the sun rises and sets, how the ocean waves flow, how the rain and snow form, how the animals live.

Since you know so much, why don't you answer my questions instead of questioning me?"

Job responded to God in Job 42:3: "Surely I spoke of things I did not understand, things too wonderful for me to know." Once Job came face to face with God, he realized he didn't need his questions answered anymore. Sure, an explanation might have been nice, just as it might be nice for us. Ultimately, though, Job realized God was bigger and wiser than he. So much bigger and wiser, in fact, Job could not possibly understand why He would work in the way He did. If Job could understand everything about God, He wouldn't be a very powerful God, would He?

When you and I face difficult circumstances that threaten to break us, we often question God, asking why He allowed such a thing to happen to us. We question His goodness and His love. At times, if we're brave, we might even voice our questions aloud. "God, how could you do this to me and still claim to adore me as your child? How can you just sit there and do nothing when I'm hurting so much? Why have you done miracle after miracle for other people but not stepped in to do one for me?"

There's nothing wrong with questioning God. In fact, the book of Psalms is full of questions for God and even in this book, in Job 42:8, God commended Job's words. There's nothing wrong with asking God our questions, as long as we understand He may — or may not — answer them.

The question is, will we be okay with the unknowns? Will we accept God's silence, when what we really desire are explanations? Will we, like Job, be okay to not understand why God allowed something into our lives?

I like to understand how things work. When I learn a new program on my computer, I want to know why I need to push a certain button or use a certain command. My husband, on the other hand, doesn't share this need. He works with technology as the creative arts minister at our church. Though he knows a lot about the inner workings of computers, sound consoles, and light boards, his main concern isn't to understand them but to make them work effectively.

When he tries to teach me things on my computer, it's often a struggle for him because I want to know why we have to push a certain key. Keith has taught me, in regards to technology, we don't always have to get it. It's okay to *not* understand something.

That's true for computers and technology, and it is true in life. Understanding our lives is good, but trusting God with them is even better.

QUESTIONS FOR REFLECTION

1. Has God ever failed to answer one of your questions? If so, please describe the situation.
2. Why do you think God doesn't answer all of our questions?
3. What helps you accept the unknowns?

PRAYER

Pray for God to help you be okay with not knowing why He allows difficulties into your life. Ask Him to help you trust in His love, even when you don't understand His actions. Pray He reminds you of His love on days when you're struggling with the unknowns.

SCRIPTURES FOR FURTHER MEDITATION

Isaiah 40:28, Psalm 8:3–4

JOURNAL ACTIVITY

Make a list of all of the amazing things about our Creator God. As you look over this list, think about how impossible it is for us to truly understand His actions. Below your list, write Isaiah 55:9, "As the heavens are higher than the earth, so are my ways higher than your ways and my thoughts than your thoughts."

TAKEAWAY

When you're searching for answers and are met by silence, learn to be okay with the unknowns.

Peter vs. Judas

Scripture reading: Luke 22:31–34, 54–62, Matthew 27:3–5

"When you have turned back,
strengthen your brothers." — Luke 22:32

I
n the middle of a painful trial, we often ask a lot of questions. Questions like… Why me? Why is this happening? Who is to blame for what I'm going through? When is this going to end? When are you going to answer, Lord? Where are you, God?

There's one question we often don't ask, but we should. That question is "Now that this has happened, what should I do?"

There's nothing wrong with asking questions. Sometimes, it's the asking that leads us into greater communion with the Father. Other times, however, we get so fixated on our unanswered questions we fail to move forward. The solution to this stagnation is to ask a different question. Instead of asking "why," begin to ask "what now?"

Let's look at Judas and Peter who handled their situations in different ways. After Judas, the disciple who betrayed Jesus, realized his mistake, he killed himself. Instead of repenting of his sin and turning back to the One who could save him, he chose instead to end his life.

Peter also betrayed Jesus. Three times, when people questioned his relationship with the Savior, Peter denied knowing his friend. Three times, when given the opportunity to stand up for his Savior, Peter chose the cowardly action — to lie about even knowing Jesus.

The difference between Judas and Peter was not in their denials. Both of them denied Jesus. Both of them broke Jesus' heart by their actions. Both of them sinned. The difference was in their reactions after the dust settled. Only one of them asked "what now?" afterward.

Judas focused on his mistake and his feelings in the here-and-now.

175

Peter chose to focus on the future. Jesus had challenged Peter in Luke 22:32 to come back after he had turned away and to then encourage the other believers: "When you have turned back, strengthen your brothers." That's exactly what Peter did. In fact, Peter went on to become the pillar for the first century church. That never would have happened if Peter hadn't thought about the future.

Sometimes I wonder how God might have used Judas if he hadn't chosen to end his life. Could God have saved Judas? I'm convinced He could have. Could God have used Judas' testimony in the early church? Again, I believe it possible. The reason God didn't use Judas' story was not because He was unwilling. It was because Judas didn't give Him the opportunity.

Judas had good reason to be broken by his sin. So did Peter. But neither of them had good reason to prevent God from using them further.

It would have been easy for Peter to focus on his mistake and on his brokenness in the moment. It might also be easy for us to do the same. Our heartbreak can seem so huge… so thunderous… so immovable. Whether our pain is because of our sin or is no fault of our own doesn't change the decision before us.

We can choose to stay where we are, stuck in our brokenness, or we can choose to look to God's future for us. Regardless of what you have done or what has been done to you or what you have gone through, I can promise you, God is *not* done with you yet. He has big plans for you, just as He did with Peter.

He has plans to use what you're going through today to change someone's tomorrow. His only requirement is your willingness. God doesn't want us to stay broken. I love the picture Psalm 147:3 paints. "He heals the brokenhearted and binds up their wounds." Can you see that? God, the very One who made the universe, gets down on one knee, lowers Himself to our level, and then tenderly wraps a bandage around our broken hearts.

In God's kingdom, broken things don't stay broken. They get fixed. God knows what He's doing, and He knows how to mend our broken hearts. He knows how to take our "what now?" and turn it into something amazing.

QUESTIONS FOR REFLECTION

1. What was the primary difference between Judas and Peter?
2. Do you think "What now?" is a better question to ask than "Why?" Please explain your answer.

PRAYER

Ask God to help you become a forward-thinking person. Pray for courage to ask "what now" instead of "why."

SCRIPTURES FOR FURTHER MEDITATION

Psalm 147:3, Psalm 30:2, Psalm 103:2–4, James 5:16

JOURNAL ACTIVITY

Write the question, "What now?" in your journal. Then, below it, brainstorm ways God might use your current struggle to change the lives of those around you tomorrow.

TAKEAWAY

When you're searching for answers, ask a better question.

ADDITIONAL NOTE

Suicide is a very real threat, among both believers and unbelievers. It does not differentiate between the poor and the wealthy, between the healthy and the sick, between races or backgrounds. Suicide unfortunately attacks a wide variety of people. If you are struggling with suicidal thoughts, please get some help. Call 1-800-273-8255 *today*. God is not finished with you yet.

The Man Born Blind

Scripture reading: John 9:1–41

*"'Neither this man nor his parents sinned,'
said Jesus, 'but this happened so that the works
of God might be displayed in him.'"* — John 9:3

E
ach time I visited my doctor for a suspected miscarriage, he said the same thing. "This is *not* your fault." It was reassuring, but also left me wondering whose fault it was. If I didn't do anything to cause this and my husband didn't do anything, then who is to blame?

It's human nature to want to place blame on someone or something. We think if we understand why something happened, we will feel better. One thing I learned is, understanding why doesn't fix the heartache.

After our miscarriages, I wanted to know why God allowed them. I thought if I understood His reasoning, it would be easier to accept the losses and move on. In reality, even if God told me why, even if He sat with me and explained in detail why He allowed each of our miscarriages, my heart would still be broken. I just want my babies back.

Sure, understanding God's reasoning might lighten the blow, but it won't bring back the children I long to hold. It won't change the past. For this reason, I have tried to stop asking why. I've tried to stop forcing blame on someone for things that can't be changed.

Unfortunately, the tendency to lay blame has been around for centuries. In John 9, the disciples asked Jesus why a man was blind. They wanted to know who caused the problem. Was it his sin, or his parents' sin? In those days, people assumed physical ailments were the result of unrepented sin.

"'Neither this man nor his parents sinned,' said Jesus, 'but this happened so that the works of God might be displayed in him." (John 9:3) Jesus heard their accusation and told them they were wrong. Neither could be blamed for the man's suffering.

I don't know the specifics that led you to this book, but I imagine you have had times you wanted to know why something happened to you. Maybe you blame yourself and think... *If only I took my child to the doctor sooner, maybe he wouldn't have died. If only I prayed more. If only I exercised more or ate better, then maybe he wouldn't have left.*

If this is you, Jesus wants you to hear His heart. Just as He reassured the blind man his ailment was not his fault, He wants you to know the same. There are some problems we bring on ourselves, but many times they have little to do with us. If we didn't directly cause our ailment, there's no reason to blame ourselves for something that was never ours to control.

Maybe you don't blame yourself. Maybe it's obvious to you and to everyone else the blame falls on someone else's shoulders. Though Jesus didn't address this situation in this text, he did address it elsewhere. In Matthew 18:21–22, in the New Living Translation, Peter asked Jesus how many times he had to forgive someone who hurt him. "Seven times?" Peter asked, thinking seven was more than generous. Jesus told him, "No, not seven times... but seventy times seven!" Jesus' point is not that we keep track and stop forgiving after we reach a certain number, but that we keep on forgiving. We never stop. If someone else caused whatever heartache you are experiencing, Jesus' answer is forgiveness.

There's one other possibility I haven't addressed yet. Maybe you know your pain is not your fault, and you know it's not someone else's fault. Since we don't have anyone else to accuse, we will lay the blame at God's feet. He's capable of preventing the catastrophe, and since He didn't, we wag our fingers at Him and cry for justice. The answer for our "why" is, God didn't step in. Why are we hurting? Because God failed to help. Who caused our pain? The One who didn't save us from it.

Please hear my heart as I write these words. Blaming God for your pain and growing bitter because of His failure to help is not going to make anything better. Believe me. I've lived it.

Jesus told His disciples the man was blind so that God's power could be displayed in him. In this particular situation, it seems God is to blame. God allowed the man to be blind so His glory could be shown through the healing. As I've thought about this, I've wondered if I would be such a willing participant of God's plan. If God wanted to use my pain for His glory, would I be willing, or would I instead seek my own happiness even if it meant God wouldn't get the glory?

QUESTIONS FOR REFLECTION

1. In your situation, have you asked why or sought to discover the cause of the pain?
2. Do you agree or disagree with the following statement: "Blaming God for your pain is not going to make anything better"? Why do you agree? Why do you disagree?

PRAYER

Ask God to help you stop seeking a cause for your pain. Pray instead He would help you move forward.

SCRIPTURES FOR FURTHER MEDITATION

Philippians 3:13–14, 2 Corinthians 5:17, Isaiah 43:18–19

JOURNAL ACTIVITY

Write and then answer the following question in your journal, "If God gets more glory from my pain than from my healing, am I willing to go through the pain?"

TAKEAWAY

When you're searching for answers and wonder who caused your pain, look forward to what's ahead instead of backwards to what's behind.

The Disciples and Paul

Scripture reading: 2 Corinthians 11:22–30, Romans 8:18

*"I consider that our present sufferings
are not worth comparing with the glory
that will be revealed in us." — Romans 8:18*

'm reading a book right now called *The Hardest Peace* by Kara Tippetts. Kara, as a 36-year-old mom of four, was diagnosed with breast cancer. Since her diagnosis, she has fought hard, along with her doctors and prayer warriors across the country. She hoped and prayed God would take away the cancer, but in the end, Kara went home to be with the Lord.[1]

Kara's husband Jason is a minister, and this is what he said in a recent sermon, "We want suffering to be like pregnancy — we have a season, and it's over, and there is a tidy moral to the story."[2] There is truth in this statement, isn't there? We want our pain and suffering to come to an end. We can handle it for a season but don't want it to go on indefinitely. Just as a midterm exam has a final question, we want our suffering to have a last page too. In effect, we want to shut the door on that part of our lives and move on to happier days.

But what if that door never shuts? What if the suffering doesn't come to an end in this life?

When we had our first miscarriage, I wasn't shocked God allowed it. But I was surprised when He allowed three more, when the pain kept going month after month and year after year. We aren't shocked when we experience some pain. We might even expect it as part of living in a fallen world. But many of us also expect it to end. We expect God to do a miracle and ride in on a horse as our Knight in shining armor. Sometimes, though, our Knight never comes and we never get our happily ever after on this side of heaven's gates.

What happens if God chooses not to do a miracle as we expect? Is it still worth it to follow Him if He won't step in and save us from our sufferings?

Kara and Jason, and I along with them, are convinced it is. Even if God doesn't answer our prayers like we want Him to, even if God doesn't heal our bodies, even if God doesn't restore our relationships, He is still good, and following Him is still worth it.

I think Jesus' disciples would say the same thing if you were to ask them today. According to tradition, Simon Peter was crucified upside down, Andrew was also crucified, James was killed by the sword, Thomas was speared to death, and John was thrown into boiling oil though not killed by this torture. Others were beaten, beheaded, tortured, and ultimately murdered for their faith in Jesus Christ.

Paul listed some of the suffering he went through. "Five times I received from the Jews the forty lashes minus one. Three times I was beaten with rods, once I was pelted with stones, three times I was shipwrecked, I spent a night and a day in the open sea, I have been constantly on the move. I have been in danger from rivers, in danger from bandits, in danger from my fellow Jews, in danger from Gentiles; in danger in the city, in danger in the country, in danger at sea; and in danger from false believers. I have labored and toiled and have often gone without sleep; I have known hunger and thirst and have often gone without food; I have been cold and naked." (2 Corithians 11:24–27)

Even though Paul experienced more than most of us can even imagine, he found joy through it all. "In all our troubles my joy knows no bounds." (2 Cor. 7:4) He was "sorrowful, yet always rejoicing." (2 Cor. 6:10) And "For Christ's sake, I delight in weaknesses, in insults, in hardships, in persecutions, in difficulties. For when I am weak, then I am strong." (2 Cor. 12:10)

Paul understood, probably more than many of us do today, what suffering felt like. He also knew Jesus was worth it. Jesus was worth every single blow, every single tear, and every single cry.

Today, I want to ask you a question: Is Jesus worth it to you? Are you willing to follow Him even if He doesn't fix your situation? Are you willing to go through the pain to receive the glory? Paul was able to have joy in the midst of agonizing circumstances because he knew what awaited him on the other side. Are you willing, like Paul was, and like Kara and Jason are, to hang on? Our present sufferings, though excruciating now, will someday be miniscule in the light of what God has prepared for us for eternity.

QUESTIONS FOR REFLECTION

1. Why do you think Jesus' followers were willing to go through such intense suffering for the sake of their belief in Jesus?
2. If you can answer that Jesus is worth all of the pain and suffering you're going through, why is He worth it for you?

PRAYER

Ask God to give you the courage to say, along with Paul and Jesus' disciples, that you will follow Him, even when the going gets tough.

SCRIPTURES FOR FURTHER MEDITATION

2 Corinthians 7:4, 2 Corinthians 6:3–10, Romans 8:18

JOURNAL ACTIVITY

Reread the questions in the last paragraph. Then take a few minutes to reflect on whether or not you really believe Jesus is worth it to you.

TAKEAWAY

When you're searching for answers and wonder if it's worth it, answer as Paul did in the affirmative. Jesus is worth it!

God the Father

Scripture reading: Revelation 21:1–5

*"He will wipe every tear from their eyes. There will be
no more death or mourning or crying or pain, for the
old order of things has passed away." — Revelation 21:4*

My boys ask a lot of questions. They ask about nature, sharks, snakes, spiders, food, our bodies, and everything in between. Even though at times I am worn down by their questions, I don't ever want them to stop asking.

I want to be the one to whom they come when they don't understand something. I want to be the one to whom they run when they're not sure if something a friend told them is correct.

My kids typically ask questions to those they are closest to. My son doesn't pelt a stranger on the street with questions. Instead, he asks my husband and me because he knows two things about us. First of all, he knows it's a safe place to ask. We're not going to get angry with him for asking. In our home, there is no question that is off limits and no topic we're not willing to discuss with him. Secondly, he asks us because he knows we'll tell him the truth. He has learned from experience we will always be honest with him.

This week, we've talked about questions many of us might want to ask God. Why does He allow suffering into the lives of His beloved children? Who is to blame when bad things happen? What do we do after our nightmares come true? Is it really worth it to follow Jesus, especially if our lives are painful and tragic at times?

There are no easy answers to any of these questions, but that doesn't mean we should stop asking. Just as I long for my children to always come to me with their questions, our heavenly Father longs for us to continue asking Him as well. David left us a great example in the Psalms of someone who came to God with his doubts. In Psalm 142:2, he said, "I pour out before him my complaint; before him I tell my trouble." David brought his questions to the One who held the answers. So did many other biblical figures. Job, Jeremiah, and even Jesus, as he hung on the cross, brought a question before His Father in heaven.

When you and I go through difficult times, we can go to God for the same two reasons my boys can come to me. It is a safe place to go, and He will always tell us the truth. He might not tell us everything we want to know just as we, as parents, don't always tell our children everything but only what they need to know at the moment.

Nonetheless, He will always listen to the cries of our hearts. He will always tell us the truth. And, even more comforting, He will always be there to collect our tears. Psalm 56:8, in the New Living Translation, says, "You keep track of all my sorrows. You have collected all my tears in your bottle. You have recorded each one in your book."

There is not one tear that has formed in the corner of your eye God hasn't noticed. Every single time you have cried, He has carefully collected each teardrop. On days when you wonder if anyone sees your pain, you can know — with certainty — God has. On days when you wonder if anyone cares about what you're feeling, you can know God does. Hebrews 10:23 says, "Let us hold unswervingly to the hope we profess, for he who promised is faithful." He who promised is faithful. He will not let us down.

Revelation 21:4 says God will wipe every tear from our eyes. On that day, when we enter the gates of the city without tears, "there will be no more death or mourning or crying or pain." Precious reader, don't allow your circumstances to keep you away from God. Keep coming to Him with your questions, your sorrows, and your tears. Bury your head into the shoulder of your Father. He may not answer all of our questions on this side of heaven, but He will hold all of our tears in His ever-loving, gracious hands. When we cling to Him, we overcome. *That* is how to be unbeaten.

QUESTIONS FOR REFLECTION

1. What questions have you had recently for God?
2. Why do we sometimes hesitate to ask God our questions?

PRAYER

Spend time in prayer today, asking God your questions.

SCRIPTURES FOR FURTHER MEDITATION

Psalm 142:2, Psalm 56:8, Isaiah 25:8, Luke 6:21

JOURNAL ACTIVITY

Reflect on the past ten weeks. How has God spoken to you through this time in His Word? Are there any points of application you want to remember? If so, write them in your journal today.

TAKEAWAY

When you're searching for answers, ask the One who knows the answers, understands your pain, and holds your tears in His hands!

Study Guide

WEEK 1: WHEN DIFFICULTIES COME

The Bible is clear we will face difficulties in this life. It's part of living in a fallen world with sinful people who do sinful things. We all know hard times will come, but they still leave us reeling. This week, we looked at the following biblical figures: Adam and Eve, Naomi, Job, Peter, Paul, and Silas.

Please watch this week's video (www.crossrivermedia.com/portfolio/ unbeaten-week-one) and then answer the following questions.

Discussion Questions

1. What are you hoping to gain from this study?
2. In the devotional about Adam and Eve, we talked about how suffering has been around since the fall. How does knowing others are struggling alongside of you affect your attitude about pain and suffering?
3. Why do you think we sometimes feel like we have it so much worse than those around us?
4. In the devotional about Naomi, we discussed how God longs to restore our lives. What are some good things you have seen God bring out of someone's difficult situation?
5. Job is the ultimate example of someone who suffered and overcame. What things did Job do that helped him overcome?
6. Peter was able to walk on water when his eyes were fixed on Jesus, but he began to sink when he looked at the waves. Why do you think it's so hard to keep our eyes fixed on Jesus in the middle of a storm?

7. What helped you look to Jesus in your pain?

8. Paul and Silas chose to sing songs to Jesus while in jail. What effect do you think their worship had on those around them?

9. What difficulty (either yours or a loved one's) led you to this devotional? As a group, spend time praying over each of the struggles mentioned.

10. What was your favorite devotional this week and why?

WEEK 2: WHEN GOD IS NOWHERE TO BE FOUND

This week, we studied five biblical figures who had good reason to wonder where God went. If these men and women played a game of hide and seek with God, He would win. What they hopefully learned is that sometimes, even when we can't find God, He's just as near as ever.

Please watch this week's video (www.crossrivermedia.com/portfolio/ unbeaten-week-two) and then answer the following questions.

Discussion Questions

1. Why do you think children love the game of hide and seek so much? Did you enjoy it as a child? Why or why not?

2. In the book of Esther, God's name is never mentioned. Why do you think the writer chose to leave it out?

3. What leads us to feel like God is absent from our lives?

4. Twice, the Israelites went through periods of silence from God. The first time was while in slavery in Egypt, the second between the Old and New Testaments. When have you felt God's silence? How did it make you feel?

5. What might be some of the benefits of silence?

6. Elisha's servant assumed he was going to die when enemy armies surrounded him and Elisha. What he failed to see was the presence of God's armies with them. Do you believe there are unseen forces at work in your life? Why or why not?

7. Jesus' disciples had a rough Friday and a devastating Saturday, but a life altering Sunday. What do you imagine were some of their emotions on each of those days?

8. What can we do when God feels distant?

9. What was your favorite devotional this week and why?

WEEK 3: WHEN GOD SEEMS LATE

There were times in the Bible when God seemed late. We looked at five of these this week: Lazarus' death, Stephen's stoning, Hannah's barrenness, Abraham and Sarah's unfulfilled promise, and Jairus' child's death. While God seemed late, each time He showed up, He brought more glory to His name than He would have if He'd shown up earlier.

Please watch this week's video (www.crossrivermedia.com/portfolio/ unbeaten-week-three) and then answer the following questions.

Discussion Questions

1. Have you ever been really late somewhere? Please describe.

2. Are you an "always late" type of a person or a "we're late if we're not five minutes early" type of person?

3. What might be some of the causes for God's apparent delay?

4. What are some of the benefits of waiting on God?

5. Why is waiting on God so difficult?

6. What are some things you can do to encourage someone else who might be waiting on God?

7. What should we do as we wait for God? Search for the song "Waiting Here for You" by Christy Nockels on YouTube and listen to it.

8. In the devotional about Stephen, the author suggested Jesus might have stood in heaven to cheer Stephen on. What types of things do you think Jesus might want to say to someone struggling in their faith today?

9. Do you think we ever take matters into our own hands, like Abra-

ham and Sarah did? What are some everyday examples of this?
10. What's the difference between God causing pain and allowing it?
11. What was your favorite devotional this week and why?

WEEK 4: WHEN GOD DOESN'T SAVE

God saves. Period. But sometimes instead of saving us from pain, He saves us through it. This week, we studied the lives of Daniel, Shadrach, Meshach, Abednego, Lazarus, Jesus, and Paul. God might not have saved these men in the way they wanted Him to, but make no mistake: God did save them, one way or the other.

Please watch this week's video (www.crossrivermedia.com/portfolio/ unbeaten-week-four) and then answer the following questions.

Discussion Questions

1. When you hear the word "save," what first comes to mind?
2. Describe a close call in your life when you or someone close to you could have been seriously hurt but wasn't.
3. Why do you think God sometimes allows us to go through painful situations like lions' dens, fiery furnaces, and thorns in the flesh?
4. We all know pain hurts, but it also has some benefits. What are some of its benefits?
5. Colossians 3:2 says, "Set your minds on things above, not on earthly things." How can a heavenly focus help you today?
6. What helps you focus on heaven throughout the day?
7. What do you imagine heaven will be like?
8. If life were fair, Jesus wouldn't have died. Nonetheless, many of us still want life to be fair. Why do you think we long for fairness?
9. What were some of the good things that might have resulted from Paul's thorn in the flesh?
10. What was your favorite devotional this week and why?

WEEK 5: WHEN BAD THINGS HAPPEN TO GOOD PEOPLE

Joseph, Jesus, Moses, Hosea, and John the Baptist had one thing in common: they didn't deserve the treatment they received. Joseph didn't deserve to be sold as a slave. Hosea didn't deserve to be cheated on. John the Baptist didn't deserve prison. Jesus, most definitely, didn't deserve death. These men had appalling things happen to them, but they learned what to do when bad things happen to good people.

Please watch this week's video (www.crossrivermedia.com/portfolio/ unbeaten-week-five) and then answer the following questions.

Discussion Questions

1. The title of this week is "When Bad Things Happen to Good People." We tend to classify people as either good or bad. Why do you think we do this?

2. What are some of the qualities we look for in a "good person"? What about a "bad person"?

3. In the devotional about Joseph, we talked about off-limit trials. What do you think are some common off-limit trials for Christians in America?

4. What are some off-limit difficulties for you?

5. What's the danger of believing God will never allow certain trials in our lives?

6. Why might God sometimes ask us to do things that are painful (like in the case of Hosea)?

7. Most Christians struggle with doubt at some point in their lives. Why do you think this is true?

8. Why do you think we sometimes feel guilty for doubting?

9. Is it difficult for you to run to God with your doubts? Why or why not?

10. What was your favorite devotional this week and why?

WEEK 6: WHEN YOU ARE STUCK IN THE SHADOWS

This week, we looked at six biblical figures who lived in another person's shadow — Rachel, Leah, Joshua, John the Baptist, David, and Hagar. Just as they might have struggled with living in the shadows, we might struggle with it too. One of the temptations of living in a social-media driven world is to feel like you never measure up. The truth is, we do measure up... not because of who we are but because of Whose we are.

Please watch this week's video (www.crossrivermedia.com/portfolio/unbeaten-week-six) and then answer the following questions.

Discussion Questions

1. What social media sites are you active on?
2. Which social media site is your favorite and why?
3. What are some of the dangers of social media?
4. What do you think is the primary cause of insecurity among Christian people today (specifically women)?
5. Why are comparisons so dangerous?
6. In the devotional about John the Baptist, we talked about famous Christians. What are some of the dangers of being known in this world?
7. What is one area of life in which you'd like to be successful?
8. How is God's definition of success different than the world's?
9. One of the best ways to combat feelings of insecurity is to fill your mind with God's thoughts of you. What does God think of you? Do you have any favorite Bible verses that help you feel more secure in His love for you?
10. What was your favorite devotional this week and why?

WEEK 7: WHEN YOU DID NOTHING WRONG

Many times we suffer, not because of things we do wrong, but because of the actions of someone else. This past week, we looked at several men who experienced pain as a direct result of someone else's actions. We studied the following biblical figures: Esau, Joseph, Elijah, Peter, and Jesus.

Please watch this week's video (www.crossrivermedia.com/portfolio/ unbeaten-week-seven) and then answer the following questions.

Discussion Questions

1. Why do we want to get even with someone who has wronged us?
2. Describe an instance in which you have felt short-changed (either from God or from someone else).
3. Do you agree or disagree we sometimes have the right to be angry? Please explain.
4. Why is forgiveness so difficult?
5. Ephesians 4:32 says, "Be kind and compassionate to one another, forgiving each other, just as in Christ God forgave you." What does forgiveness look like in everyday life?
6. In the devotional about Peter, we talked about the link between rest and trust in God. How is trust related to rest?
7. Jesus did more than just forgive His enemies. He also prayed for God to bless them. Why is it hard to pray for those who have hurt us?
8. Write a name on a piece of paper of someone you need to forgive. Then pray for this individual throughout the week.
9. What was your favorite devotional this week and why?

WEEK 8: WHEN YOU ONLY HAVE YOURSELF TO BLAME

Sometimes, other people cause our pain. Other times, we bring it upon ourselves. Jonah brought pain upon himself when he despised God's mercy poured out on another, the sinful woman brought it upon herself when she acted out her temptations, and the envious servants did so when they were ungrateful for the payment they received. We also inadvertently cause our own suffering sometimes.

Please watch this week's video (www.crossrivermedia.com/portfolio/ unbeaten-week-eight) and then answer the following questions.

Discussion Questions

1. How do you think most Christians react to someone who is caught in sin? Why do you think they react in this way?
2. What was Jesus' reaction to the woman caught in adultery?
3. Why do we sometimes hesitate to offer the same grace to others that Jesus has offered to us?
4. Do you believe some sins are worse than others? Why?
5. We are all sinners, and yet we often act like our sins aren't as bad as the sins of another. Why do you think we do this?
6. In the devotional about David, the author stated that God is more interested in our holiness than our happiness. Why do you think this is true?
7. What are some ways God might discipline us?
8. What is the difference between discipline and wrath?
9. Why is gratitude so important?
10. What are three things for which you are thankful today?
11. What was your favorite devotional this week and why?

WEEK 9: WHEN THE FUTURE ISN'T CLEAR

The future can be terrifying, especially when we have no idea what lies ahead of us. This past week, we studied the lives of several people who learned to trust God with unknown futures. We read about Abraham and Sarah, the Israelites as they wandered through the desert, the Proverbs 31 woman, the mother of Jesus, and John.

Please watch this week's video (www.crossrivermedia.com/portfolio/ unbeaten-week-nine) and then answer the following questions.

Discussion Questions

1. If you could have complete control over your future, what would your life look like in five years? Describe it.
2. Do you think it would be a good thing or a bad thing if we could control our lives completely? Explain.
3. Why is the unknown so frightening?
4. If we knew exactly what the future held, would we even need faith? Why or why not?
5. Would you have been able to do what Abram and Sarai did? Why or why not?
6. Why was the Proverbs 31 woman able to laugh at the days to come?
7. What do you do when God doesn't seem to be leading you anywhere? What is your default?
8. What character traits have you developed through detours?
9. What do you most fear about your future?
10. Is it possible to fear God and fear the future at the same time? Why or why not?
11. What helps you *not* fear the future?
12. What was your favorite devotional this week and why?

WEEK 10: WHEN YOU ARE SEARCHING FOR ANSWERS

No doubt about it, there will be times we don't understand the things that are happening to us or to our loved ones. In moments like these, we might have questions for God. We might wonder why He seems silent, who caused the pain we are going through, or if it's really worth it to follow Jesus. In this final week of devotionals, we asked the hard questions, right alongside Job, Peter, the man who was born blind, Paul, and Jesus' first disciples. My prayer is you found comfort in their stories and maybe even a little hope to get you through a difficult season.

Please watch this week's video (www.crossrivermedia.com/portfolio/

unbeaten-week-ten) and then answer the following questions.

Discussion Questions

1. Kids ask a lot of questions. Why do you think this is true?
2. When is it hardest for you to bring your questions to God?
3. Why do you think God sometimes chooses not to answer all of our questions?
4. How were Judas and Peter different in the way they responded to their sins?
5. In the devotional about Peter, the author encouraged you to ask "What now?" instead of "Why?" Think about this question as it relates to whatever you're going through now. What might God want you to do now?
6. Why do you think we have such a tendency to place blame on someone when things go wrong?
7. What are some of the dangers of placing blame on someone when something bad happens to us?
8. What was your favorite devotional this week and why?
9. What is one thing you have learned or been reminded of through this entire study?

FROM THE AUTHOR

Writing about pain and suffering is not an easy task, but it's one I'm honored to be able to do, and I pray I've done the topic justice. Thank you for allowing me to share my heart through this devotional, and thank you for sharing yours. Notes from readers are what keep me writing. If you'd like to get in touch with me, please connect through my website at www.lindseymbell.com

Endnotes

WEEK ONE

1. Secondary infertility is infertility that a couple experiences after having one or more successful previous pregnancies.

WEEK 2

1. *NIV Life Application Study Bible* (Tyndale House Publishers and Zondervan Publishing House, 1991).
2. Jennifer Rothschild, *God is Just Not Fair: Finding Hope When Life Doesn't Make Sense* (Grand Rapids, MI: Zondervan, 2013).
3. You can watch a short video about our miscarriages and adoption here: http://www.youtube.com/watch?v=eyUmcXTsLQc

WEEK THREE

1. Dillon Burroughs, *Hunger No More: A 1-Year Devotional Journey Through the Psalms* (Birmingham, AL: New Hope Publishers, 2012).

WEEK FOUR

1. John Groberg, *The Other Side of Heaven* (Salt Lake City: Deseret Book, 1993).
2. I owe this concept to two different women: Beth Moore and Jennifer Rothschild.
3. I owe this terminology to Jennifer Rothschild and her book *God is Just Not Fair*, published by Zondervan in 2013.
4. "Standing in the Presence of the Almighty" by Robin Sigars, quoted in *Scripture to Live By* by Aaron Chambers (Avon, MA: Adams Media, 2007), 135.

WEEK FIVE

1. This poem was reportedly found etched on the walls of a concentration camp. Author unknown.

WEEK SIX

1. Read more from Steven Furtick at his website: http://stevenfurtick.com.
2. Jennifer Dukes Lee, *Love Idol: Letting Go of Your Need for Approval and Seeing Yourself through God's Eyes* (Carol Stream, IL: Tyndale, 2014), 218.

WEEK 7

1. Jennifer Rothschild, *God is Just Not Fair.*
2. Not all who struggle with insomnia also struggle with trusting God, but I do. My sleep, or lack of sleep, is directly related to the amount of trust I place in God.
3. To listen to Laurie Coombs' testimony, follow this link: http://lauriecoombs.org/media/
4. Max Lucado, *Before Amen: The Power of a Simple Prayer* (Nashville: Thomas Nelson, 2014), 80.

WEEK 8

1. www1.cbn.com/books/saving-a-serial-killer

WEEK 10

1. Between the time this book was being written and the time it was released, Kara Tippetts passed from this life into the next. Please pray for her husband and children.
2. Kara Tippetts, *The Hardest Peace* (Colorado Springs, CO: David C. Cook, 2014), 97.

LINDSEY BELL

Lindsey Bell is a chocolate-loving speaker and author from the Midwest. Her love affair with Jesus began when she attended vacation Bible school with a friend in junior high. It was there she learned about a God who adored her and wanted to have a relationship with her. She gave her life to Christ as a teenager and has been living for Him ever since.

Lindsey and her husband, Keith, were high school sweethearts and have been married for more than a decade. After graduating from Ozark Christian College, they began serving together in the local church, where they are still serving today.

When she's not writing, Lindsey loves to dig into new books (especially if she's also sipping on a Cherry Coke), enjoy a chocolate chip cookie, or go for a walk around the neighborhood. One of her favorite things to do is to cuddle on the couch with her two car-loving, ornery boys that Lindsey is lucky enough to stay home with. Keith and Lindsey also have four children they look forward to meeting in heaven someday.

www.LindseyMBell.com
www.Facebook.com/AuthorLindseyBell
www.Twitter.com/LindseyMBell

GENERATIONS

What happens when God steps in to change one man's life?

CR CrossRiver Media
www.crossrivermedia.com

MORE GREAT BOOKS FROM CROSSRIVERMEDIA.COM

BETHANY'S CALENDAR
Elaine Marie Cooper

One minute Bethany Cooper seemed fine — the next she was strapped to a gurney in the E.R. diagnosed with a terminal brain tumor. During the next few months, her mother Elaine Marie Cooper used her nursing skills to not only help Bethany battle an unseen enemy, she also learned to recognize the hand of God on her daughter's life. *Bethany's Calendar* is a story of fear and faith, commitment and compassion, told with gut-wrenching honesty while sharing unwavering faith in God. (SELAH Award, 2015)

CARRIED BY GRACE
Debra L. Butterfield

A family member… a friend… someone you know has sexually abused your child. Tumultuous emotions buffet you from all sides. You're feeling lost and confused. Where do you turn for help? Part memoir, part devotional, author Debra L. Butterfield offers comfort for your heartache, practical guidance for daily needs, a biblical path to healing, and encouragement and hope along the way. Let yourself be *Carried by Grace* as you journey toward restoration.

THE BENEFIT PACKAGE
Tamara Clymer

Love, redemption, mercy, provision, revelation and healing… In Psalm 103, David listed just a few of the good things God did for him. His list gives us plenty to be thankful for during tough times. No matter your circumstances or background, God is always full of compassion, generous with His mercy, unfailing in His love and powerful in healing. When circumstances overwhelm you — unwrap the *Benefit Package* and rediscover God's goodness.

THIS I KNOW
Toby Holsinger

Author and teen, Tobi Holsinger, has discovered that while the Bible was written 2000 years ago, our heavenly Father has some great advice and insight on some of the toughest stuff teens face including rape, gossip, suicide, and peer pressure. Whatever you're facing, God understands and His Word holds answers, compassion, and encouragement. Grab your Bible and a pen and get ready to take a fresh look at God's Word. (2014 CSPA Book of the Year)

The
Grace
Impact
a devotional

How God's grace covers every aspect of our life.